Education
begins at
Birth

A Parent's Guide to Preparing Infants, Toddlers, and Preschoolers for Kindergarten

---

Jeff Wiesman, Ed.D.
&
Annie Wiesman

Acknowledgements

We would like to express our appreciation to those who played a key role in making this book possible. We especially wish to thank Wendy Connell for offering many helpful insights and comments. Your suggestions were highly valued and they greatly enhanced our book.

A special thanks to Jane Miner for your assistance with research and for helping us to refine many ideas. We also wish to show our gratitude to Michael Christopher for his editorial review. Thanks for sharing your expertise while addressing our countless questions.

To Blake, Eric, and Sandy; we are grateful for your support along the way. Finally, to Allie, thank you for all that you teach us. We learn as much from you as we hope you learn from us.

Contents

Introduction

Why This Book?

As a former kindergarten teacher and parent of a toddler, Annie is often approached by other parents wondering how they can prepare their young children for kindergarten. Moms and dads regularly ask questions such as, "What are some things I can do to develop my toddler's skills?" "What type of academic content should I teach?" "Do you know of a curriculum I can follow?"

As a college professor who instructs future elementary school teachers, I (Jeff) regularly think about curriculum and effective teaching strategies for young children. Based on the questions we heard from parents, the knowledge we've gained in our teaching careers, and our experiences with our daughter, we decided to write this practical, user-friendly guide.

Whether you are a single parent, a stay-at-home mom or dad, or in a household where both parents work, this book is designed to help you prepare your infants, toddlers, and preschoolers for kindergarten. There is a host of parenting books out there, but here are reasons why this one will be helpful as you strive to set your children up for success.

- We focus on developing the whole child—body, mind, character, and social-emotional growth. Preparing your little one's cognitive abilities for school is only one facet.

We also include ideas and strategies for developing a positive temperament and raising well-rounded children.

- We include many fun and engaging activities you can do with your kids.
- In just about all cases we suggest free or very inexpensive ideas for families on any budget.
- Our book reinforces and provides information about how to enhance many of the things you are probably already doing.
- The suggested teaching practices are grounded in research, but written in simple-to-follow language.
- The academic content we recommend teaching is based on state and national standards for preschoolers.
- We have numerous years of teaching experience and have studied child development for decades.
- While the Internet certainly offers a plethora of information, we include all you need to know to successfully raise smart kids and prepare them for kindergarten. Our book includes developmentally appropriate strategies— all neatly packaged in the pages that follow so you won't have to spend hours searching for curriculum and teaching activities.

In short, we provide guidance regarding what you should teach your pre–kindergartner, how you should teach the content, when it is appropriate to introduce each concept, and reasons why you should apply the ideas we suggest. When you focus on the fundamentals included in our book and create a culture of learning in your home, your children will be ready for kindergarten. You will develop a strong foundation that will not only help them to succeed in school but also in life.

1

Setting Your Little One up for Success

Parents have an incredible opportunity to help children learn foundational knowledge and skills during the first several years of life. All infants (0 – 12 months), toddlers (12 – 36 months), and preschool-aged children (3 – 5 years) are acquiring, organizing, and processing information. Caregivers simply need to nurture these naturally occurring processes.

By incorporating thoughtful activities and providing opportunities for growth, you will develop confident and knowledgeable kids who will succeed in school. Without a doubt, your involvement and life experiences can increase your children's cognitive development, abilities, and skills.[1] As you continue to read the pages of this book, we plan to equip you with numerous ways to maximize their potential.

Since the 1960s the United States Department of Education has stressed the importance of providing young children with an opportunity to start off on the right foot. Millions of dollars have been spent on government initiatives related to preschool education, because kids often lag behind in kindergarten. Those who struggle in elementary school simply may not have learned foundational knowledge and skills before the age of six. Often, parents ask kindergarten teachers what they should be doing to help their children start strong in school. While that is always a good question to consider, preparing for kindergarten really should start much sooner, even during infancy. Of course, it is never too late to start building a strong foundation, but it does help to start earlier rather than later. In addition, it is important for parents to realize that they may already be doing things that have excellent educational value. They simply need to build and expand upon naturally occurring events and experiences.

There are numerous ways parents can formally get involved with their child's education to enhance learning during the early years. However, we also want to encourage families to allow their kids to be kids. The founder of kindergarten had a goal to create a space where young children would engage in social activities, exercise their bodies, and learn through observation and experience.[2] A famous educator, Maria Montessori, agreed with this mindset and said a preschool student's environment "must be rich in motives which lend interest to activity and invite the child to conduct his or her own experiences."[3]

Current educators also express concern about the rigors of the 21st century curriculum at the kindergarten level. There are fewer opportunities for play and, instead, an increased focus on academics. Specifically, math and literacy content have been heavily stressed, and other content areas such as art, music, science, and child-driven experiences have been devalued.[4] The best way to set your little one up for success is to realize the power of play and provide multiple experiences in all subjects.

How do babies, toddlers, and preschoolers learn?

Simply put, babies, toddlers, and preschoolers learn through interactive play. With young children, play and learning go hand-in-hand and active engagement will foster development in all areas—cognitively, physically, socially, and emotionally.[5] For example, kids learn problem solving skills while playing with blocks. They learn about science when playing in the sand on the beach. They learn fine motor skills when dressing dolls.

In fact, developmental psychologists have determined that when caregivers play with their toddlers and stimulate their minds through discussion and experiences, children are likely to earn higher grades in math and reading when they are in the fifth grade.[6] Here are some of the other benefits of frequent play with your child.[7]

- **Babies and toddlers learn hand-eye coordination and develop muscle coordination.** Reaching and grasping for objects, moving a toy from one hand to another, hitting a balloon into the air, and manipulating beads on a necklace all help to develop key physical functions.
- **Play promotes social skills.** When your child plays "dress-up" with friends, he or she learns how to share, take turns, and navigate through disagreements at the same time.
- **You will promote early vocabulary development during playtime.** Your children will learn terms such as first, last, forward, on top of, taller, and many other positional and directional words because we naturally use them while playing. Kids will also learn hundreds and hundreds of nouns, adjectives, and other words when engaging with toys.
- **Children's understanding of cause and effect will increase when playing.** As babies, they discover that a toy will make a sound when they squeeze it, and an object will drop to the ground when they let go of it.
- **When parents play with their kids, everyone has an increased sense of joy and fulfillment.** Touching, smiling, and sharing a good laugh are all great medicine for the mind and body.
- **Play will enhance kids' attention span and their ability to persevere in difficult situations.**

Provide as many different experiences as you can for your children. Perform investigations together about color, size, texture, and weight of objects. Schedule play dates with other parents. Be a part of a group to develop a sense of belonging. Provide opportunities to help and serve others.

Have many conversations and ask questions about your child's environment. What does she observe? What does she like? What does she dislike? How was her day? What was her favorite part of the day? These types of discussions will help to intellectually engage and challenge your preschooler.

We must constantly communicate with our kids. The more words they hear by age four, the better prepared they will be for kindergarten. In fact, pediatric professor Dr. Dana Suskind determined that some children hear 30 million fewer words than others in the early years. Those who hear fewer words often start and stay behind in school. Conversely, children who hear more words have a better vocabulary, are better readers, and earn higher test scores by third grade.[8]

The diagram below provides a helpful summary of things parents can do to create an environment where infants, toddlers, and preschoolers will learn.

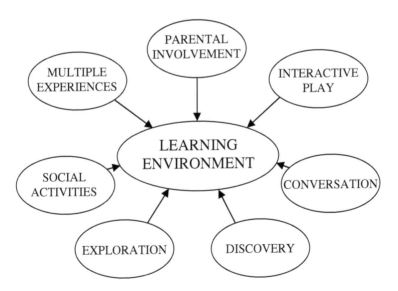

I (Jeff) know it can sometimes be an exercise of patience and perseverance. I often come home from work tired, or I don't want to take the time and energy to engage and converse with our daughter. Sometimes, I am simply lazy or selfish—I would rather do something else. But through continual activity and exposure, young children will learn. It is a very logical progression: The more kids engage in play and conversation the more they must use their brain, which then leads to increased cognitive growth.

What is the parent's role when kids are playing?

If you are wondering how to engage during your child's play, professor of early childhood education, Dr. Fiona Baker, offers suggestions. Play time should be adult-led, but then caregivers should create space where children can use their imagination and be creative.[9] For example, a parent may provide a toddler with a set of blocks, and the parent simply sits with the child, engages with him, shows interest, and asks questions.

The parent is a guide and resource—the child does the exploring, discovering, and learning. Provide assistance only when necessary, be a good listener, teach your children to be good listeners, and create a culture of inquiry and thought.

However, this doesn't mean that all play needs to be interactive. There is value in independent play for children of all ages. Even babies benefit from solo play time during the day. Children build autonomy, independence, and confidence when playing alone for a period of time each day. But remember, this time is still parent-directed in that the caregiver is establishing a safe space and providing developmentally appropriate toys to manipulate, discover, and explore.

The reality is that all kids have lively minds. No matter your economic status, geographic location, family heritage, race, ethnicity, or household situation, your child is curious and eager to learn. The key is to start early!

Learning begins at infancy, and it is often as simple as talking to your little one. Continual conversation with your children in the first three years of life strongly links with their IQ and language skills later in life.[10] So engage your infant by reading books to her, or by describing daily activities. As soon as your child is able to speak words, dialogue about the events in your family's life. It will make a difference.

What does it mean to be smart?

Parents will help children succeed if they stress two types of learning. The first type is considered academic learning. This includes knowing the ABCs, counting, identifying common geometric shapes, and learning other basic facts such as color names and body parts. To best teach academic knowledge, we should take an interdisciplinary approach. For instance, kids can start to learn letters while talking about scientific concepts, or they can learn how to count when reading a book.

The second type of learning involves the development of cognitive functions, which include problem solving, critical thinking skills, and the ability to reason, process information, and make good decisions. You will see that we stress both types of learning in this book. We develop cognitive functions while we incorporate engaging activities and teach subject-specific content.

Kids who are able to learn on their own tend to be successful in the classroom. You can help children take control of their learning by helping them to create and define goals. Think about the tools needed to accomplish the learning tasks, and then monitor your preschoolers' thinking and progress. Offer guidance, encourage them to evaluate their actions, and come up with possible alternatives if something isn't working as planned.

When our daughter was three years old, she wanted to make a fort with chairs, a box, and a blanket. The blanket kept falling off the chair (thus ruining the fort) so we asked her to think of strategies and other objects she could use to keep the fort together. She brought in an additional chair and some pillows and she was eventually able to build a pretty solid fort. Ask your kids what they want to accomplish and then let them take initiative with their own strategies and solutions.

You will build self-confidence by attributing your children's success to hard work, by following through with a good plan, and by getting excited about their achievements. Praise them in a way that highlights their ability to learn, think, and grow. Be specific with feedback like "I think your fort worked well because you put a pillow on top to hold the blanket in place."

Comment on the thought processes and specifically state why something was effective. However, it is important to avoid over-praising. Kids will develop confidence only when praise is warranted. Focus on their strengths, provide opportunities to improve on weaknesses, and if you are intentional with your words, this type of focus will translate to greater academic success later in school.[11]

Meeting the needs of young children

It is important to note that, before children can maximize learning, parents must first consider their basic needs. Therefore, strive to provide healthy meals and establish an early bed time to ensure a good night's sleep. Don't underestimate the importance of adequate sleep for early mental and physical development.

Create a loving, caring, and safe environment in which your kids feel free to ask questions and take responsibility. A young child's brain will develop when parents show affection and demonstrate love through words and actions. As an added benefit, this type of care in the early years will in turn help children handle stress and process information more effectively later in life.[12]

Help them work through fear and unpredictable circumstances with conversations and nurture. A television sitcom called *Last Man Standing* included an episode in which a young boy no longer felt confident trying new things because his parents were always afraid that he would get hurt. The parents did not properly address issues of fear with the boy, and he eventually stopped taking risks altogether. His potential for growth was stunted in a very humorous way. Even though the show exaggerated his lack of confidence, it did accurately stress the importance of meeting kids' needs.

Remember that each child is different and will learn best according to his or her unique personality and learning style. Some kids will prefer to learn visually while others might prefer to have discussions. Some will be more strong-willed and others will be more laid-back. Some toddlers will be ready to learn earlier than others. Take these differences into account and work with your children's strengths and weaknesses.

Finally, you will maximize learning potential if you continually teach and revisit content with varied educational experiences. We offer dozens of teaching ideas and activities throughout this book. Make it a point to do them multiple times throughout your preschooler's life to help develop a strong working memory of the skills and ideas.

What hinders development and cognitive growth?

While there are many things parents can do to help nurture children, there are also some situations to avoid. Certainly, no parent is perfect. There are times when we all do things that might impede growth, but it is especially important to consider the following.

Avoid high pressure learning environments
Sometimes preschool providers and parents create a climate in which kids are pushed to higher standards than appropri-

ate. In other words, let young kids learn through fun, exploration, and experience more often than through structured learning environments.

Don't underestimate kids' intellectual potential

While it is important to consider developmental capabilities (which we will discuss in a later chapter), try to challenge your children with complex thoughts and ideas. One's intelligence is not a fixed trait, so develop a mindset that intellectual growth can occur with anyone.

We all learn with exposure, effort, struggle, and failure, and we must avoid statements such as "Our family has never been very good at math," or "Daddy never liked reading." Instead, model a growth mindset and teach your little one that learning is limitless and should be life-long.

Use technology wisely

The wrong type of play might actually hinder growth and learning. For example, if play refers to a game on a computing device such as a tablet or phone, then kids likely won't be learning, especially if they are playing in isolation. There are other negative influences of technology that may or may not be obvious. Sometimes the presence of television and other technological devices decrease the quality and quantity of parent-child interactions.

Because too much screen time can stunt development, the American Academy of Pediatrics recommends avoiding screen media for children younger than 18 months (with the exception of video-chatting with family and friends).[13] For toddlers between the ages of 18 and 24 months, parents should watch high-quality programming with their children to help them understand what they see. For two- to five-year-old kids, limit screen time to one hour per day. Again, caregivers should view media with them and use it to extend and apply knowledge.

When you are able to make connections with an educational app or a TV program, to something they have experienced or learned, then technology is especially useful. Interact with the technology and your kids: Sit with them, ask questions, and build on what is seen on the screen.[14]

Try to minimize the chaos

Sibling quarrels, instability of routines, loud electronic devices, and some of the occurrences of family life have a tendency to be chaotic, don't they? While some amount of chaos is inevitable, studies have linked household chaos to decreased learning and a poorer attention span in preschoolers.[15] Do all you can to shield your little one from the craziness. Try to build in a quiet time each day and include routines where all devices are off and family members are reading, talking about the day, or playing a game together.

If you understand how young children learn and avoid environments that hinder growth, then you can build a solid foundation. Intentionally interact with math, reading, science, and social studies content with your kids. Teach critical thinking and problem solving skills and provide opportunities for them to develop artistically and physically. Educational experiences don't always have to be structured, but it is important to take early action. The next six chapters offer information regarding the academic content you should teach, and how an education can begin at birth. Purposely include the suggested activities and ideas and your children will be ready for the challenges of school.

2

Math: It's as Easy as 1, 2, 3

When parents are able to help their toddlers and preschoolers develop math abilities, kids will be more likely to do well in mathematics later in school.[1] In other words, early childhood instruction is essential for later success. Interestingly, early math knowledge also transfers into other content areas—it has an impact on reading and science skills.[2]

So when can you begin talking about numbers and geometry with your little ones? Children as young as 18 months old begin to learn fundamental concepts.[3] They may not develop complete understandings that young, but their little brains are able to begin to think about math ideas.

To help build a foundation, one of the most important things you can do is foster a positive attitude. In fact, according to one survey, about 30% of the American population would rather clean toilets than do math problems![4] Be careful not to pass on this mindset or any of your own phobias.

Instead, talk about how math is useful and worthwhile and then work diligently to instill confidence. There are volumes of articles that discuss how kids often don't think they can be good at math. Without a doubt, this type of mentality has the potential to limit growth. Also avoid believing in the myth that some people can do math and others cannot. While some might have more natural mathematical abilities and inclinations, all can be successful with effort, time, and when utilizing the proper strategies.

How do young children learn math?

As with any subject, one of the best ways to develop an understanding of math is to simply have conversations. Make note of geometric shapes when you take a walk around your neighborhood. Point out the rectangular road signs, the circular window on someone's house, or any other shape you see. Compare the size of different objects in life. Talk about what a bigger number means when you read a thermometer. Count your fingers or toes. It also helps when kids are able to get their little hands on objects and play with items they can manipulate.

Objects around the house often represent mathematical ideas. When playing with blocks, children learn relative size and how to sort. When using Play-Doh, kids can create geometric shapes. Parents can use coins to expose toddlers to numbers. Additionally, manipulatives often create scenarios where kids must problem solve and develop fine motor skills. For instance, stacking a series of blocks might require strategy and the ability to accurately position pieces.

Other ways to effectively help toddlers and preschoolers learn math include reading age-appropriate story books with numbers or shapes. (*Counting Kisses* by Karen Katz does a great job of connecting math with everyday life.) Finally, when you play games, create drawings, and make crafts, take the opportunity to talk about patterns, shapes, and numbers.

State and national standards stress the importance of thinking mathematically and they focus on describing geometric shapes in space, counting, comparing sets or numerals, and learning vocabulary related to math.[5] In the sections that follow, we include the specific topics and concepts you can teach your preschooler along with strategies that will help turn your child into a math whiz.

Counting and numbers

As the title of this chapter suggests, teaching your kids how to count isn't a difficult task. And you might be surprised to know that children as young as two years of age have the ability to accurately count one, two, or three objects. Parents simply need to be aware of five main counting principles preschoolers must learn.[6] In addition to the principles, your child should start to recognize numbers with your assistance. Keep reading for a more detailed description of each concept.

Can your child recite the numbers?

Children's first experience with math often begins with small numbers. In fact, as soon as they can start talking they are able to recite numbers. They won't understand what the numbers actually mean until the ages of two to three years old, but they can begin to memorize the order of the numbers quite early in life. This principle includes developing an understanding that numbers are always used in a fixed order (one, two, three, four, etc.) when counting objects.

When we drove in the car with our two-year-old daughter, there were probably hundreds of times when we counted to ten with her. As she was learning, she often forgot to include certain numbers and we would simply state that four always comes after three or five comes after four. With this type of practice, she eventually mastered counting to ten.

Then we would practice counting to 20 together, and by the time she was three years old, she was able to recite the numbers up to 30. Just about all kids will begin to learn the numbers with this type of rote memorization.

Did your child skip any or count some twice?

The second principle toddlers can begin to master relates with the idea that each item is to be counted once and only once. This is called the one-to-one correspondence principle. It is interesting to watch children count a set of five objects for the first time when they are about two years old. They will either count the same one twice or forget to include an object in the set.

A great strategy to help with this principle is to count the fingers on your hand. As your little one counts each finger, put it down so it transfers from the "to be counted" category to the "already counted" category. Another helpful strategy is to line up whatever you are counting. Instead of counting buttons randomly placed on a table, line them up in a row and your child will find more success.

If you start practicing this concept early, children as young as three are developmentally able to master this.[7] We started teaching this to our daughter when she was two, but it took her at least a year before she excelled at it.

How many objects are there?

This principle—called the cardinal principle—simply states that when you count objects in a set, the last object you count is the same as the total number of objects in the set. As kids learn math, they might correctly count seven blocks on a table, but if you ask, "How many blocks are there?" immediately after counting, they often answer incorrectly or begin counting the objects again. This is normal and it is simply something you must stress. For example, after counting seven blocks state, "That means there are a total of seven blocks on the table."

Similarly, toddlers and preschoolers might make the following mistake: If you ask your child to show you seven blocks, she might point to the last block as opposed to pointing to the whole set. So you'll want to emphasize that the last number reached when counting tells us how many objects are in a collection of items.

How many total objects are there?

Children learning to count will often have a difficult time counting different objects within the same set. For instance, if you had a picture containing four cats and three dogs, you must teach your child that the animals can be counted together, giving you a total of seven. In other words, differing kinds of objects can be counted together in a group. This is called the abstraction principle, and as with many other math principles, kids will master this idea with practice. Here are a few other ideas connected with everyday life.

- Count the number of girls and boys in your house and then ask how many total people are in the family.
- Count the number of forks and knives when setting the table and then see if they can tell you the total amount of silverware on the table.
- Count pennies and dimes and state the total number of coins.

Does order matter?

This idea is known as the order-irrelevance principle, and it stresses that the order in which objects are counted does not matter as long as the other counting principles aren't violated. While counting the number of fingers on my hand, I would ask our daughter to count from pinky to thumb and then count again going from thumb to pinky. She quickly discovered that we counted a total of five fingers both ways.

Can your child recognize the numbers?

You want your two- to three-year-old children to begin to recognize written numbers. Just as they learn what an oval or square looks like, help them learn to identify numbers. Start with one through nine, and talk about the defining attributes of each number. Kids will struggle distinguishing a "6" from a "9," but you can point out characteristics such as how "8" has two circles or how "1" has only a single, straight line.

Counting activities

Below includes a list of activities to help kids recognize numbers as well as master the five main counting principles. These are all appropriate for preschool students and they will certainly be fun and engaging.

Number cards   Age: 1½ − 2½
Skill Development: Number recognition; recite numbers
Directions: Start by creating one set of number cards and putting them in order. Point to each number as you count. Then create a second set of the number cards, mix them up, and practice matching while placing them in order (start with matching the "1" cards together, then the "2" cards, and so on). Similarly, you could clip magazine or newspaper pictures that show numbers in big print and then place them in order. Simple activities like this help with number recognition more than you might think.

1	2	3	4	5
1	2	3	4	5

Counting to...   Age: 1½ − 4
Skill Development: Recite numbers; one-to-one correspondence
Directions: Count everything in your child's world—fingers, trees, chairs, books, blocks, or chips. Start with numbers under five and touch each item as you count them. If possible, line the items up or put them in a rectangular array to help with one-to-one correspondence. When you ask your child to count, allow her to continue until she makes several errors. Make note of the types of errors she makes: Number sequence errors? Skipping items? Counting items more than once? Also, while you are taking a walk, waiting in line at the grocery store, or driving to a friend's house, simply encourage your child to count out loud—ask him to count to five, or ten, or to whatever number he is able. This is something you

can do at just about any time, and this type of repetition is helpful.

Number & item puzzle   Age: 2½ – 4
Skill Development: Number recognition, one-to-one correspondence
Directions: Create, print, and cut out two sets of cards, one with the numerals and the other with the corresponding number of items on it. Mix them up, and then ask your child to match the picture card with its numeral while laying them in order. Using different shapes will help teach geometry, too.

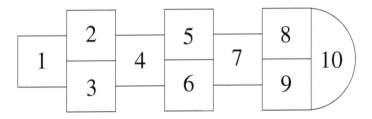

Hopscotch   Age: 2½ – 6
Skill Development: Number recognition; recite numbers
Directions: Use sidewalk chalk to create a hopscotch board on your driveway or sidewalk. As your child hops on each number, count with him. He probably won't be an expert hopscotcher early on, but this game will develop basic counting skills while enhancing gross motor skills at the same time.

Clothespin number match   Age: 3 – 5
Skill Development: Cardinal principle; recite numbers; number recognition

Directions: Use cardstock or index cards and write numbers 1 through 9 on them, one number per card. Then work with your child to count and clip the correct number of clothespins on each respective card. Instead of using clothespins, you can use coins or chips and place the correct amount on each card (but kids tend to prefer the clothespins and they help with fine motor skills).

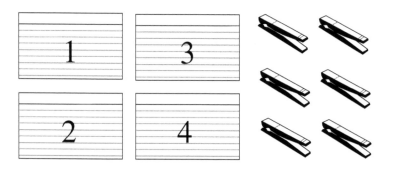

Counting puzzles   Age: 3 – 5

Skill Development: Recite numbers; number recognition

Directions: Print out a picture of a favorite animal or object and subdivide it into ten pieces as shown below. Sequentially number each piece, cut out along the dotted lines, mix them up, and then ask your little one to put the puzzle together. As your child gets better with counting, make a new puzzle with more pieces.

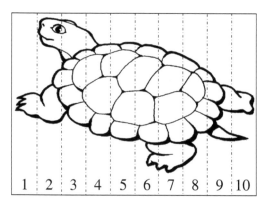

Five & ten frames   Age: 3 – 5

Skill Development: One-to-one correspondence

Directions: On a piece of paper, create a 1 x 5 rectangular array and use chips, coins, or other objects that will fit in the squares. Place one chip in each square and count as you go (the example below and to the left is a picture representation of the number three). Once they have mastered numbers that fit in one five frame, create a ten frame (as shown on the right) and count numbers up to ten.

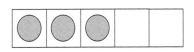
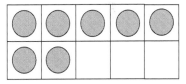

Inside & outside   Age: 3 – 5

Skill Development: One-to-one correspondence; abstraction principle

Directions: On a large piece of paper, draw a circle and place some pennies inside and some outside the circle. Ask your preschooler to figure out how many are inside and how many are outside. Then ask her to identify the total number of pennies. Repeat with varying amounts of pennies.

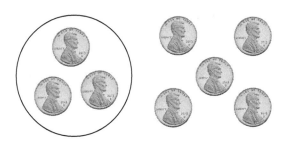

Counting on   Age: 4 – 6

Skill Development: Recite numbers

Directions: You will need a die and coins for this activity. Start by placing a small amount of coins on a flat surface, and then roll a die. Start with the number you roll and count on from there. As an illustration, if you roll a six and have three coins on the table, your child would start at 6, and then say, "7, 8, 9."

Writing numbers   Age: 4 – 6

Skill Development: Writing; number recognition
Directions: Use crayons, markers, sidewalk chalk or any other fun writing utensil to aid your child's ability to write numbers. Start by tracing numbers using the recommended stroke pattern seen below. Then see if she can copy them below the given numbers. After she masters tracing and copying, see if she can write them in order from memory.

Geometry

When kids draw, play with objects, and look at pictures, they begin to learn about geometry—which is simply the study of patterns, shapes, sizes, positions, and spatial relationships. Geometry is relevant in many areas in life. Artists, engineers, builders, and architects are a small sampling of people who regularly use related principles in the workplace. And we all apply geometry with activities such as decorating, gardening, construction, and design.

An important first step to any geometric or educational toy is to first give it to your child and let her explore and discover without any direction or input. Observe what she does with it, how she holds it, and how long it keeps her attention. An infant chewing on a plastic colored ring is exposed to important information. What does it look like? How does it feel? Does it make a noise?

As she grows older, you can ask open-ended questions about what she sees, notices, or feels. Guide her to try different things before explicitly teaching a certain concept. Additionally, don't be too quick to assist or correct your child when manipulating objects. Let her discover mistakes and solve problems. For instance, if she is trying to stack rings in order based on size, but puts them out of order, make guiding comments only after she plays for a while.

Infants, toddlers, and preschoolers start to learn about geometry simply by recognizing different shapes. Toddlers won't be able to understand specific properties and relationships among shapes, but they will compare everyday objects. In other words, they can identify a rectangle and recognize that a door is in the shape of a rectangle, but won't be able to discuss the differences between a rectangle and a triangle.

Kids closer to four or five years old will begin to understand the basic properties of geometric shapes and develop the ability to compare and contrast objects. They will be able to distinguish between two- and three-dimensional shapes, learn vocabulary related to differing properties, and identify spatial relationships. The specific geometric concepts children must learn include shapes and spatial reasoning.

Shapes

Introduce your infant to various geometric shapes early and often. Create or purchase an inexpensive set of basic objects including circles, squares, triangles, hexagons, ovals, and stars. Begin by stating the name of each shape. Through regular exposure, your toddler will eventually be able to name them on his own.

Once your child is developmentally able (usually at around four or five years old), compare, contrast, and draw various shapes. See if he can trace over an existing picture. If able to do that successfully, encourage him to draw shapes on his own. Playing with sidewalk chalk is a fun way to develop this ability.

Provide time for your toddler to play with, manipulate, and rotate the shapes. Explain how some always look the same in different positions (circles and squares) while others might look a little different when they are rotated (hearts can be upside down). In addition, ask your child to sort and classify a set of multiple shapes and stress that a square will always be a square regardless of its orientation, color, or size.

Once he has mastered the introductory shapes, slowly introduce others, such as rectangles, parallelograms, octagons, and pentagons. As you introduce new two-dimensional shapes, continue to name, compare, contrast, sort, trace, classify, and draw them.

Another way to enhance kids' understanding of geometric objects is by playing with a tangram puzzle. A tangram is composed of seven pieces that can be arranged to form various shapes. Most tangram puzzles consist of two larger triangles, one medium-sized triangle, two small triangles, a square, and a parallelogram.

Tangram Puzzle:

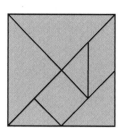
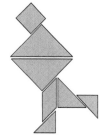
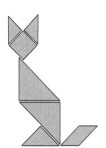

Not only can you talk about the different shapes, but you can also help kids understand relative size (small, medium, and large) and develop spatial understandings. By moving pieces around and rotating them, children will be better able to recognize the relative position of objects.

I (Jeff) was able to find a free app on my phone. Our daughter loves playing with tangrams, and as early as age three she was able to solve the easier puzzles. You could also create your own set at minimal cost, using card stock and a ruler.

Spatial reasoning

As we mentioned, tangrams help to cultivate another important mathematical ability, namely one's spatial reasoning. Child psychologists believe spatial reasoning starts to develop as early as six months old, and it is defined as one's ability to understand patterns, directions, distances, and relative locations of objects.[8]

When children play with tangrams, they learn to position objects next to each other and think about what happens when shapes are rotated. For example, depending on how you rotate and position two triangles, you can form a larger triangle. If you place them differently, you can create a square or parallelogram.

When you move shapes you build vocabulary, since you use descriptive language such as up, down, to the side, the other side, and next to. When you place tangram pieces together you are also creating composite shapes, another important math standard for pre-kindergarten kids. By comparing, describing relative positions, and introducing these basic ideas and concepts, you are developing process skills that are vital to early math development.

Another fun activity is called "I-Spy." This game is easy to incorporate while driving or taking a walk around the neighborhood. When in a setting where many signs and objects are visible, say something like, "I spy with my little eye a rectangle." Then your toddler looks around and finds an object that is in the shape of a rectangle (such as a street sign or a picture on the side of a truck). Kids get very excited when they find various shapes and they will proudly declare, "I see it!" This activity fosters an understanding of the shapes around us and it connects geometry with children's ever-expanding world.

When your child is about a year or two away from kindergarten there are a few more advanced geometric concepts that are appropriate to introduce. First, you can explain how some shapes have symmetry by folding or cutting them in half. Simply show your preschooler how one half looks exactly the same as the other.

Second, talk about some of the basic properties and differences among two-dimensional shapes. For instance, a rectangle has straight sides and circles have curved sides. A square has four sides and a hexagon has six sides.

Finally, introduce three-dimensional shapes such as cones, cubes, and spheres. Keep it basic and discuss how two-dimensional shapes are flat and three-dimensional shapes are not.

Geometry activities

One of the best ways to engage your children with geometric ideas is to complete crafts with them. While doing just about any type of craft, you can discuss geometric shapes and increase spatial reasoning. When playing with Play-Doh or Wikki Stix, you can also encourage your child to make designs and model shapes. (Wikki Stix are sticky, bendable sticks that can be formed into two-dimensional or three-dimensional shapes. They are safe to play with and you can buy a set of them for under $10 at Amazon or Walmart.)

Here are a few more activities that will help develop geometry skills.

Blocks   Age: 1 – 5

Directions: Start by allowing your little one to simply stack blocks (whenever they are developmentally capable). As an extension for older children, draw three-dimensional patterns on index cards and see if your child can create a matching pattern using the blocks. Be sure to begin with simple patterns.

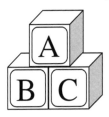

Sorting shapes   Age: 2 – 5

Directions: Create or purchase an inexpensive set of geometric shapes that include at least six or seven different shapes in a variety of colors. Then see if your child can sort them by color and by shape. (We found a set that included a hexagon, square, oval, triangle, circle, heart, and star in four different colors.) Be sure to state the name of each shape—or ask if your child knows the name—as you sort.

Geoboard   Age: 3 – 5

Directions: You can purchase a Geoboard online for under $10, or you can use an app. For the hands-on version, find some rubber bands and start creating shapes.

Algebraic thinking

Your preschoolers will start to think algebraically as they begin to master the counting principles. Then you will foster algebraic thinking by:

- Discussing number relationships (five is bigger than three).
- Talking about how numbers will change in different situations (if I invite another friend to the party, I need one more cup).
- Helping children to recognize patterns.
- Introducing addition by combining or putting objects together (if you start with two red M & M's and you combine them with three blue M & M's, the total number of M & M's changes).
- Introducing subtraction by taking away objects.

While your toddler or preschooler doesn't have to completely understand these algebraic ideas, she will begin to comprehend these important concepts with experience.

At one point, when our daughter was three years old, we had four pieces of pancake cut up and we asked her, "How many pieces would I have left if I ate one?" She was able to answer three. Thinking that her answer might have been a fluke, we tried it again. "Okay, now we have three pieces, how many will be left if I ate one." Again, she answered correctly.

Since she had a visual with the pancakes, we thought we would try it without the visual (the entire pancake was eaten at this point). So we asked, "What if I have six bites on my plate and I ate one?" To our surprise she was able to answer correctly without actually seeing it.

You can also model subtraction by separating subsets of a whole. For instance, if you have a set of eight chips, where three are red and five are blue, talk about how many chips remain if you take away the blue ones.

There are a few other algebraic ideas you can easily practice with your preschoolers. Ask them to identify the next number of a given number (What number comes after five?), or ask what comes before a given number (What number comes before seven?).

"Counting on" is another skill that educators ask kindergartners to master. Count to ten, but instead of starting at one, start with three. Mix it up and start with different numbers.

Finally, use objects or drawings to decompose numbers. In other words, ask your child to find the number you would need to make a given total. A great way to practice this concept is with your fingers. If I have two fingers pointed up, "How many more fingers would I have to move so all five are up?" "What if I have four fingers pointed up, then how many more to get all five?"

As an additional example, after collecting candy at Halloween, ask: "If I have two pieces of candy, how many more pieces of candy would I need to get a total of three pieces?" These ideas are difficult for some kindergarten students to understand, but they won't hurt to try with your three- to five-year-old children.

Thinking mathematically

The previously mentioned skills and strategies are vital, but perhaps the most important thing you can do to prepare your child for math is to get her to *think* mathematically. This includes teaching "life skills" such as identifying patterns, exploring, comparing and contrasting, problem solving, and making sense of numbers.

Identify patterns
Use people, everyday objects, and numbers to help your child sort and recognize patterns.

- What comes next in the pattern below?

- When toddlers put toys away or return clean silverware to the drawer, they develop an ability to sort.

- Make patterns and fun designs with toys and stickers.
- Order from small to large using toys or stuffed animals (one is small, the second is medium, and the third is large).

Explore math-related topics

Begin to expose your children to concepts such as measurement, money, puzzles, and time.

- Use a tape measure to determine the height of family members and of your child's doll collection. When we started doing this with our daughter at age three, she had no idea what a measurement indicated, but she started to learn to put one end of the tape measure by our feet and then extend the other to our heads.
- Complete simple jigsaw puzzles (which will also help develop spatial awareness and reasoning).
- Measure objects using other objects. For example, a pencil is eight pennies long, or twelve dominoes fill up the area of a square.
- Explore and use measuring tools such as scales, cups, and teaspoons. Whenever you bake cookies or cakes with your toddler, use that opportunity to introduce different forms of measurement.
- Talk about concepts related to time. What does tomorrow or in a few minutes mean? What's the difference between morning and night? How long is a week or a month? Indeed, these concepts are pretty abstract for preschoolers and pretty difficult for them to comprehend, but exposure is still beneficial.

Compare and contrast

Make comparisons with the many objects that are a part of your toddler's world. Compare the size of animals such as mice, squirrels, and deer. Compare the size of different people in terms of who is taller or shorter. Contrast heavy items with lighter items. Also, it would be helpful to teach your preschooler to describe the relative position of different objects. Is the square above or below the triangle? Is the car inside or outside of the garage? Is the pine tree in front of or behind the house?

Problem solve

Teach your child to solve problems with everyday tasks. Whether your little one is trying to figure out how to button a shirt or open a Tupperware container, allow him to struggle with the task a little. For sure, offer suggestions, but give him a chance to solve the problem on his own first. Encourage him to stay calm and avoid getting frustrated. Ask helpful questions and discuss different strategies. When preschoolers are able to solve everyday problems, they develop a skill that will carry over into math problems they might face in kindergarten and beyond.

Make sense of numbers

Nurture the development of number sense, which you can do with children as early as age two. In math education, number sense is defined as a person's ability to understand number relationships, use numbers in everyday situations, and make sense of what numbers and symbols mean.[9] You help develop number sense when you:

- Use visual images, such as pictures or symbols, to represent numbers. Seeing a pile of 5 pennies might help kids to understand that 5 is a smaller number as compared to a pile of 25 pennies.
- Encourage math conversations. Continually ask questions such as, "How many spoons?" "Which is more?" "How do you know?" "What's one more?" "What's one less?" "About how many steps to the door?" "How long do you think the drive will take?"
- Compare numbers and objects. A great way to do this is by playing the card game, "War." Remove from a regular deck of playing cards the aces and face cards (kings,

queens, and jacks) so you are left with number cards 2 through 10. Deal these remaining cards between you and your child, giving each an equal amount. Leave cards face down and at the same time, both players turn over the top card. The player with the highest number wins both cards. If there is a tie, set out three cards face down and then place the fourth card face up. The one whose fourth card is the highest gets to keep all ten cards. The game is finished when one player has all the cards or a predetermined number of cards.

- Use the five frames (we included an example of this in one of the counting activities).
- Let your children share their thoughts and strategies when exposed to a variety of math related experiences.

When kids are able to develop number sense, the benefits are many. It will promote confidence in their math abilities, help them to flexibly think about math problems, and it will lay a foundation for the more advanced mathematical ideas they will face in high school.[10]

Math standards for preschool children

While state and national standards often vary, the list below suggests when you might introduce each concept and skill. Children are expected to master all of these competencies by the time they complete preschool or kindergarten, but as you will notice, parents can start teaching children many mathematical ideas quite early.

Remember, if your children aren't mastering something, don't worry; they simply might not be developmentally ready. Have patience, keep working with them, give opportunities to practice, and they will eventually catch on. It is also important to note that these are general guidelines only—each child will learn at his or her own pace.

Birth – 12 months

During this age, parents should:
- Count with infants—count ears, eyes, toes, and fingers.
- Play with two- and three-dimensional shapes alongside children.
- State the names of the various shapes (e.g., squares, circles, and rectangles) while playing.
- Read board books with limited text that focus on counting (Sandra Boynton's *One, Two, Three!* is a great example of this type of book).

12 – 24 months

Your children should begin to learn to:
- Count orally up to 10 (recite the numbers).
- Sort and classify objects by size, shape, and color.
- Name basic geometric shapes.
- Discuss how shapes can have different sizes (e.g., a small triangle versus a big triangle).
- Make model shapes using Play-Doh, sticks, and other objects.

2 – 3 years old

Your children should begin to learn to:
- Count orally up to 30 (recite the numbers).
- Count a set of 10 objects with accurate one-to-one correspondence.
- Match sets of objects with its number, from 1 through 9 (see the activity entitled, "number and item puzzle").
- Count to tell the number of objects in a set.
- Identify whether the number of objects in one group is greater than, less than, or equal to the number of objects in another group (start with groups with less than 9 objects in each).
- Classify and count objects in different categories (see the activity entitled, "inside and outside").

- Model addition by combining two or more sets of objects.
- Model subtraction by separating and taking away subsets of a whole (e.g., if you have a set of 8 chips, where 3 are red and 5 are blue, talk about how many chips are left if you take away the blue ones).
- Identify patterns using people, objects, and numbers.
- Practice moving shapes in different directions (such as with tangrams).
- Compare, trace, draw and sort two-dimensional shapes.
- Identify and describe shapes at home and outside.
- Describe the relative position of objects in space (e.g., on, above, below, inside, outside, in front of, and behind).
- Make comparisons (e.g., taller, smaller, more, less, heavy, light, long, and short).

4 – 6 years old

Your children should begin to learn to:
- Count orally up to 50 (recite the numbers).
- Count a set of 25 objects with accurate one-to-one correspondence.
- Count forward beginning from a number other than 1 (e.g., count to 10 starting at number 3).
- Identify and write numbers from 0 to 25.
- Compare two numbers between 1 & 10 presented as numerals (What is bigger, 5 or 3?).
- Recognize that each successive number refers to a quantity that is one larger.
- Write a numeral for a set of less than 10 objects.
- Identify the next number less and the next number more than any named number.
- Recognize how combining 3 blue chips with 2 red chips gives you the same total number of chips if you were to combine 2 red chips with 3 blue chips (this is the commutative property; it doesn't matter in which order you

combine the chips, either way you end up with 5 total chips).

- Demonstrate symmetry by tracing, cutting, and folding shapes.
- Identify and compare two-dimensional and three-dimensional shapes.
- Compose basic shapes to form larger shapes (e.g., put two triangles together to form a rectangle).
- Define weight, area, time, length, and volume.
- Recognize pennies, nickels, and dimes.
- Measure objects with non-standard objects (e.g., a pencil is 5 paper clips long).
- Explore and use measuring tools (e.g., cups, rulers, and scales).
- Collect and organize simple data into categories (e.g., sort and count nickels, pennies, and dimes).

Making connections

As you work with your child to meet these learning outcomes, make connections with everyday life and with other subject areas. Connect math with literature by listening to and telling number stories. Play counting games like Hi-Ho Cherry-O, The Sneaky Snacky Squirrel Game, or even make up your own counting game. Find number songs on YouTube and sing them together. Find apps on your device to provide visuals. Draw pictures and make diagrams to represent geometric ideas. Count the number of leaves on a small branch and then talk about related science concepts. All of these types of multifaceted approaches will enhance your child's ability to be successful in math.

Keep in mind that there is often a connection between a parent's disposition towards math and the child's attitude. If you have some math anxiety, try not to convey the idea that you—or your children—struggle at math. Instead, be confident that you can teach it and your child can learn the topics included in this chapter. All it takes is some effort and persistence. Start during the early years to build this foundation and you will indeed raise a math genius!

3

Science: Explore & Discover the World

To be good at science doesn't only mean someone is able to regurgitate scientific facts. It is much more than that. Being an accomplished scientist also includes understanding how and why things work.[1] Yes, start by teaching your toddler factual knowledge: Trees have bark, birds have wings, and all living things need water. But don't stop there. Talk about how trees have bark for protection, how birds use their wings to thrive in their environment, and why we need fluids in our body.

You will also foster scientific thought if you teach your preschooler how to apply the scientific method. In other words, kids will maximize their knowledge and abilities when they are able to ask questions, observe, reason, and experiment.[2]

The best way to teach science to toddlers and preschoolers is through discovery, hands-on activities, and discussion.[3] Young kids like to make observations, explore relationships, and make sense of their world. As parents, we simply need to take advantage of our children's natural curiosities and their desire to understand scientific ideas. In fact, children begin to engage with their environment and develop basic understandings of scientific phenomena as early as the infant months.[4]

Here are some ways you can create early experiences.

- **Make connections.** Help your little one understand that science is all around us. Just as humans need water to survive, so do trees and plants. We put on a coat to keep warm, just like a bear "puts on" a thick coat of fur.
- **Read children's books about science.** There are many out there and simple exposure will build vocabulary and knowledge. (*Pumpkin, Pumpkin* by Jeanne Titherington is an example of science in literature—it wonderfully shows the life cycle of a pumpkin seed.) Be sure to take the time to compare the illustrations in the books with experiences and observations in nature.
- **Use pictures that represent scientific ideas.** Don't forget to include plenty of factual details with each picture.

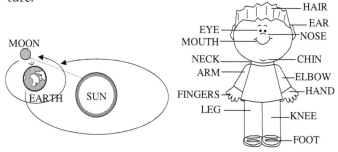

- **Engage in science experiments.** Plant flowers, observe small insects, and roll a ball down a hill. There are many more ideas to come in this chapter.
- **Take advantage of your everyday experiences.** They are often loaded with science. When you walk in a park or forest, talk about the different types of trees and listen to the sounds of the birds. If you have a chance to go to the beach, talk about the waves and tides. Go to a nature center—many are free. Our local center had a display on butterflies and our three-year-old daughter learned much about the stages of life. (It was also pretty cute to hear her pronounce chrysalis at that age.)
- **Use and talk about scientific tools.** Experiment with magnets, scales, thermometers, eye droppers, measuring

devices, and magnifying glasses. When your toddler is developmentally ready and able to do it safely, let her handle materials and equipment. We like to bake in our home, so we often use tablespoons and measuring cups. Not only do we develop an ability to use scientific tools, but we often practice counting in situations where we need multiple cups of a certain ingredient.

- **Discuss how many things change on a regular basis.** Plants and people grow, water levels in rivers and lakes change, the moon looks different at night throughout the month, weather changes seasonally, and leaves turn color.

Exposure to scientific concepts before kindergarten will create a foundation with which kids will build upon for subsequent development. And there are six main reasons why it is important to do these things early.[5]

1. Science experiences will inspire learning and increase kids' natural curiosities.
2. You can help your child develop a positive attitude toward science and create confidence.
3. This foundation will help kids learn more abstract ideas in the future.
4. You will encourage scientific thinking (more on this in the next section).
5. Exposure to science will help with other life skills, such as collecting data, organizing information, and applying ideas.
6. Scientific thinking will transfer and benefit your child in other academic areas.

On the other hand, poor science instruction in the early years might lead to negative attitudes and performance problems later in middle and high school.[6] You also want to be sure your kids aren't developing misconceptions related to scientific concepts and ideas. Kids often have a tendency to develop misguided theories based on their daily experiences.[7] For instance, toddlers might think the moon is a source of light or come to believe bigger objects are always heavier than small ones. In addition, they have difficulty understanding the difference between living and non-living things. Children sometimes think clouds are living things because they move, but plants aren't alive because they don't (except on windy days, perhaps).

In fact, parents often have the same tendency to misguide children. For example, on a cold winter day, many have asked their kids to put on a coat so they won't catch a cold. Of course, people don't necessarily catch a cold because they aren't dressing warmly enough. Instead, colds are caused by viruses that are spread from others.

We were once taking a walk on a beautiful sunny day with a handful of small puffy clouds in the sky. And our three-year-old asked, "Why are the clouds white?" Instead of answering correctly, we answered with a cute, fun, and made-up response. Even though she wouldn't necessarily understand the concept of light and reflection at that age, we ran the risk of creating a misconception that might cause confusion later in school.

More than probably any other subject area, science teachers face hurdles in class because they often have to spend a lot of time debunking misconceptions.[8] So try not to tire of the "why" questions your children ask. And don't appease them with made-up answers. Even if you think your child is too young to fully understand a scientific concept, give the correct answer using age-appropriate terms and language.

Scientific thinking

Not only is it beneficial to teach scientific concepts and facts, but it is equally helpful to foster your child's ability to think scientifically. Kids will develop the best foundation when you teach facts while cultivating skills, such as making predictions, identifying patterns, and classifying.[9] Below we have listed numerous types of thinking that will help in science.

Observation skills

From birth, infants can begin to use their five senses to make observations. As toddlers, you can ask what they see, hear, smell, taste, and touch. (Obviously, we should be careful—we don't want children touching hot stoves or putting toxic substances in their mouths.) Kids can use the senses to assist and guide learning, develop scientific understandings, and identify properties.

To illustrate, toddlers will learn about the many different types of trees by simply feeling the bark. Encourage accurate and detailed observations. Is the bark soft, crumbly, smooth, bumpy, hard, sharp, dry, wet, patterned, or sticky from sap? Scientists make these types of observations regularly and our kids can learn this skill with proper guidance.

Comparing and contrasting

When our daughter was three years old she observed a bird and a plane in the sky while we were out on a walk. That provided an opportunity to compare and contrast the two objects (they both fly but planes don't flap their wings). Regularly engage in the same types of conversations about similarities and differences among objects, toys, and daily events.

Classifying

While comparing and contrasting items, also ask your toddler to classify based on common themes or characteristics. Sort coins, colored chips, pictures of objects, stuffed dolls, and plastic animals by size, texture, color, or any other attribute of interest.

Modeling

When you and your children create models using clay, drawings, Play-Doh, pipe cleaners and just about any other material, you help them to better define scientific concepts. As a result, draw a picture of a tree and include detail of the roots, trunk, branches, and leaves. Use Play-Doh to create the major body parts of a human or animal. Dress up a doll based on different weather conditions. These types of multisensory representations will help you to better explain concepts, and you will foster your child's ability to model in science classes later on.

Hypothesizing and predicting

A prediction is a guess as to what might happen. A hypothesis is a possible explanation of something you observe. Let me (Jeff) illustrate with an example. Our three-year-old daughter and I were once playing with a small rubber ball and a Nerf football. I asked her to predict which ball would bounce higher. She was wrong with her prediction, but after bouncing both balls at the same time, I asked her to make a hypothesis as to why the football didn't bounce as high. She guessed it didn't go as high because it was softer, which was a pretty astute explanation.

When reading a book, see if your child can guess what's going to happen next. Then ask why he thinks that way. When outside, ask your son if he thinks mommy can pick up a large boulder. Then ask why mommy might or might not be able to pick it up. When you ask questions such as these, your kids will be able to draw more and more conclusions based on their experiences and observations.

Thinking about and analyzing ideas

While cleaning up one afternoon, our four-year-old had a lot of toys and a couple of kid-size chairs to put away. She was trying to carry multiple things at once, but she was getting frustrated because toys kept dropping. So we asked her to think of alternate ways to get her toys back to her room. We offered an idea and then let her determine the best course of action. After successfully getting the toys back, we evaluated the results and inquired about why it worked. This same process applies to science. If a plant isn't growing, think about solutions to help make it grow. Make a decision based on scientific knowledge and then evaluate the results.

Cause and effect

There are all sorts of cause and effect relationships in the scientific world. When there isn't much rain, the grass gets brown and it isn't as soft to play on. When it snows, sidewalks and driveways get slippery. When you touch a hot item, your skin burns and it hurts. Intentionally talk about causal relationships, and then be sure to explain why things happen.

These are just some ways in which you can begin to teach your child to think scientifically.[10] We provide more examples as we introduce the three predominant branches in science: Earth science, matter and energy, and life science.

Earth science

Weather is one component of Earth science, and it's certainly relevant because it affects what we might wear and the types of activities in which we engage. We experience it on a daily basis, so it is easy to talk about its many components, including sunlight, wind, snow, rain, temperature, fog, and storms. If it's a rainy day, explain why you aren't going to go to the park. Look at a radar map and point out what the different colors indicate. (In the winter, our toddler had the hardest time understanding how blue on a radar map meant snow because, as she said, "snow is white.")

If it's a windy day, watch the clouds move in the sky, spin a pinwheel, fly a kite, or observe how tree limbs and leaves shake. If it's sunny, discuss how the sun keeps us warm, why we might want to sit in the shade on an especially hot day, and how shadows are created.

Teach your preschooler about some of the different types of clouds—cirrus, cumulus, and nimbus clouds are three major types. Describe how each looks, and then explain how some are likely to produce rain.

Our child's grandparents live outside of Portland, Oregon, so we have an opportunity to talk about fog and rain when we visit. Because we live in a different state, we have been able to point out how different regions often have different weather patterns.

As the months go by each year wherever you live, foster an understanding of the four seasons by making connections to your family's experiences. The leaves change colors in the fall, we wear gloves in the winter, and we play in a warm creek in the summer.

Weather is closely linked with the water cycle, which is another system you can teach your preschooler. You can melt an ice cube or boil water to observe and discuss the different states of water. In the northern part of the United States, you might experience a precipitation day where rain changes to ice or snow (or vice versa).

Also identify and compare the different kinds of bodies of water, such as rivers, streams, lakes, puddles, and oceans. Take a walk in a park near lakes and streams and talk about the differences. Then teach your toddler the various uses of water. Animals need lakes to drink from, and humans use water not only to drink but also to wash themselves. At the same time, point out how we can be wasteful if we don't turn the faucet off when we are finished. This is only one way we can teach our children to protect our planet. Talk about why we should avoid littering, why we reuse clothes and pass them on to friends, or why we turn off the lights when we leave a room.

Two more topics related to Earth science include geology and basic astronomy. Kids will play in the dirt and sand, throw rocks, and ask about the mountains and hills. Simply take the time to describe each geological element, and talk about distinguishing characteristics.

Explain the basics of the sun, moon, and stars. When outside at night, point out how the moon moves throughout the sky and reflects the sun's light. The next section includes additional ideas and activities that will foster scientific knowledge related to some of the Earth's systems.

Earth science activities and experiments

Picture representations   Age: 3 – 5
Science Skills: Modeling; analyzing ideas
Directions: Use crayons or colored pencils and draw pictures of each season with your child. Be detailed and descriptive as you draw and color. Here are some ideas.

- Summer: Green leaves and grass, bright blue skies with a few puffy white clouds, people outside playing, farms growing corn and beans.
- Fall: Leaves turning colors on the trees and falling to the ground, pumpkins on the porch, wind blowing flags, grass turning brown.
- Winter: Bare trees, lawns and bushes covered with snow, footprints in the snow, snowmen in the yard, people dressed up in warm clothes.
- Spring: Flowers blooming with many colors, grass turning green again, birds flying through the air, dark clouds with rain and rainbows.

Rocks for toddlers   Age: 3 – 5
Science Skills: Observing; comparing and contrasting
Directions: This activity provides an opportunity for you to teach kids how to describe objects using their senses. Walk in the woods—ideally near a lake, creek, or river—and collect five to six different types of rocks. Let your preschooler examine the rocks and then compare and contrast by asking:

- What color are the rocks? Do certain rocks have more than one color?
- Are they smooth or bumpy?

- Are they brittle or difficult to break?
- Can you write on your driveway or sidewalk with the rock (like chalk)?
- Do they have shiny, sparkly minerals in them?

Make a cloud   Age: 4 – 5
Science Skills: Observing, modeling, cause and effect
Directions: Find a large, clear container with a lid, tape a piece of black paper to one side and fill it about a third of the way with hot water. Then light a match, blow it out, drop it into the container and quickly close the lid. Place a small bag of ice on top of the container and then observe what happens inside it. A cloud should form and be visible against the black background. You can then introduce your preschooler to many scientific principles.

- The hot water evaporates into water vapor (just as the sun heats water).
- The ice on top represents the cold air high in the sky.
- As the water vapor rises, it reaches the cold air and condenses (the vapor turns to water droplets).
- Clouds need dust particles to form (which the match provides).
- Clouds form when many water droplets cling to dust particles.
- When clouds have a lot of water in them, they produce rain.

Matter and energy

Matter can be defined as any physical substance or material that takes up different forms and properties. Parents should use descriptive language when kids play with objects and talk about size, shape, softness, weight, color, and whether something is rigid or flexible. There are so many scientific terms caregivers can introduce!

Take it a step further and investigate which types of objects will float while taking a bath or washing dishes together in the sink. After trying a couple together, see if your child can guess if different objects will float or sink. Prekindergarten standards also recommend talking about what materials are made of, including plastic, metal, fabric, wood, and rock. In your kitchen alone, you might have wood cabinets, a metal stove, plastic utensils, or countertops made of rock.

You can also cultivate an understanding of some of the forces your preschooler experiences in life. Kicking a ball will change the direction of it. Kick it harder and it will go faster and farther. If two balls collide they will push one another and change directions. Push a merry-go-round and it'll keep moving after you stop. When you let go of a bouncy ball, it will drop to the ground because of gravity. Then it will keep bouncing because it's rubbery. But if you drop a rock, it won't bounce because it's rigid.

Intentionally talk about these things while playing with your children and you will enhance their scientific knowledge. Here are a few more terms related to energy that you can get them to think about.

- Teeter totters, scissors, and many other tools are examples of **mechanical forces.**
- Children can discover and learn about **suction** by holding a cup to their mouth and breathing in.
- Buy a set of inexpensive **magnets** and show how they can make things move without touching them.
- Explore **heat and cold.** Ice will melt faster in the hot sun than in the shade, food heated from a microwave will cool down, and steam from food is hot.
- Discuss different **chemical and physical changes.** What happens when you bake a cake, mix powdered Kool Aid to water, add food coloring to frosting, melt butter while cooking, combine paint colors, and add crackers to soup?

- Identify the difference between **pushing and pulling.**

Below includes some more activities related to forces and matter that you can easily do with your children.

Matter and energy activities and experiments

Properties of matter   Age: 3 – 5
Science Skills: Observing; classifying
Directions: Gather a set of about eight everyday objects. Start by selecting two or three and describe specific properties of each one. Include descriptive language such as heavy or light, large or small, hard or soft, big or small, round or square, and any other properties you can identify. Then select a specific attribute, such as hardness, and sort all eight objects as either being hard or soft. Pick a different attribute and then re-sort objects accordingly.

Magnetic attraction   Age: 4 – 5
Science Skills: Classifying; observing
Directions: Use a refrigerator magnet or purchase an inexpensive one from the store. Collect about ten to twelve objects, some that are magnetic and some that are not. Objects such as coins, paper clips, cans, plastic and metal silverware, blocks, rocks, and bolts are easily collected in most households. Test to see which objects are magnetic and then classify them accordingly. Extend it further by seeing which can be picked up by the magnet. See if your child can figure out why the magnet won't pick up the heavier objects.

Ramping up with gravity   Age: 4 – 6
Science Skills: Hypothesizing; cause and effect
Directions: Use a long board, ruler, or piece of hard plastic and prop it up so it is at an incline. Roll various balls and round objects down the ramp and compare the time they take to get to the bottom. Add friction by laying a piece of fabric

over the ramp and then repeat with the same objects. Here is what you can discuss while conducting the experiment.

- Why do the objects roll down?
- Why do some objects take longer to get to the bottom than others?
- If we were to race two different objects, which do you think will get to the bottom first?
- Why does the fabric slow the ball down?
- What happens if you change the angle of the ramp?
- What happens if you give an object a push at the beginning?

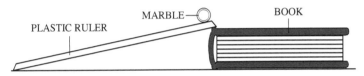

Life science

Young children love to learn about animals, plants, and the human body. Parents usually introduce basic terms and ideas related to the life sciences, but it is also important to go deeper. For example, when you walk by a tree, teach your child about its structure. Explain how roots absorb water and nutrients, the bark protects the tree from damage and disease, and the leaves provide food. Additionally, talk about the basic life cycle of a plant—the stages are so much fun to observe.

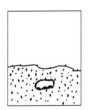

In the first stage, plant a seed in a clear, plastic cup with your children. In the second stage, the roots will grow down and a stem will sprout. Finally, more stems will emerge and leaves will grow. At the same time, have conversations about all the different types of plants and trees in your neighborhood. Make observations and comparisons. How are they similar in height? How are they different in color? What do the leaves look like? How do they smell? Do they produce fruit?

Any type of gardening with children is wonderful too. During the harvest season, take your kids to a farm and let them pick blueberries, pumpkins, or apples. Discuss the specific places where plants live. Some need to live in open fields in a place that gets a lot of sun, while others live in the water. Then extend the learning to include humans and animals. People live in buildings, bears live in a den, birds in a nest, and worms in the ground.

As you talk about humans and animals, point out all the major body parts on your child and then compare those with different animals. People have legs to walk just like a tiger and an elephant. But a tiger has a tail for balance and an elephant has a trunk to graze for food.

Notice patterns on animals—zebras have stripes and cheetahs have spots—but stress how differences do exist among the same kind of animal. It is also enjoyable to teach about animals and their offspring during the toddler years. Use the correct names for baby animals (e.g., instead of calling it a baby cow, call it a calf) and talk about how offspring will look similar to their parents.

Connect life science with personal hygiene and healthy, safe living. Discuss safety rules and potential hazards, such as a boiling pot of water, a moving car in a parking lot, or a messy room with toys to trip over. Teach and model proper behaviors such as wiping a runny nose and coughing or sneezing into your arm to avoid germs on your hands. Always encourage kids to wash their hands after going to the bathroom and brushing their teeth after meals.

Along with personal cleanliness, identify disease prevention techniques and healthy eating habits. Then teach about the interconnectedness of science and our bodies. When we drink milk, we get protein to grow strong bones. When we eat fruits and vegetables, we get energy and important nutrients to fight against disease. When we get lots of rest, we will have even more energy. When we drink plenty of water, our muscles will work better. To be sure, all humans and animals need certain types of food and nutrients to grow big and strong.

Below are some activities and experiments you can do to further enhance your little one's understanding of these life sciences.

Life science activities and experiments

Three-piece puzzles   Age: 2 – 4
Science Skills: Observing; comparing and contrasting
Directions: Search the Internet and find pictures of sequencing events representing an animal or plant's growth over time. As you see in the example below, you could complete this puzzle with an egg, an egg that is cracked, and finally a chick coming out of the egg. A second set can represent the life cycle of a butterfly, from caterpillar to chrysalis to butterfly. Cut out about five groups of three (forming 15 pieces), mix them up, and then put the three-piece puzzles together.

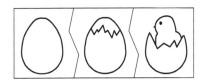

Here are some other life cycles you might consider incorporating.

- Seed to stalk to flower
- Larva to pupa to beetle
- Seedling to thin tree to mighty oak
- Tadpole to tadpole with legs to frog
- Baby to young child to adult

Where's my baby?   Age: 2 – 4

Science Skills: Analyzing ideas; predicting

Directions: Find pictures of baby animals and their mommies and daddies on the Internet or in books from your local library. Copy the pictures or print them out. Mix them and see if your toddler can identify the pairs. You can do the same with animals and their habitats. Cut out a picture of a sky and another of a bird, a fish and a river, a frog and a lily pad in a pond, a bear and a forest of trees, a desert and a snake, and a picture of a tree and a squirrel.

COW	CAT	PIG	SHEEP
CALF	KITTEN	PIGLET	LAMB

Living or non-living?   Age: 3 – 5

Science Skills: Classifying; comparing and contrasting

Directions: Find about ten pictures of living and non-living things from the Internet or a magazine. Print or cut them out and categorize into the two groups with your child. Compare and contrast each group, asking, "What makes something alive?" Then provide a definition (living things breathe, move by themselves, grow, and reproduce).

Plant growth variables   Age: 4 – 5

Science Skills: Analyzing ideas; cause and effect; observing

Directions: Buy a bag of planting soil and a packet of seeds. (We have had success planting radish seeds. They germinate quickly—in about five days—and are quite hardy. Broccoli and green beans are relatively quick to sprout as well.) Using six to eight plastic cups, fill each one about halfway with soil, place two to three seeds in the middle, and cover with more soil. Then experiment with different variables. Give two cups plenty of water but put one in the sun and one in the shade. With two others, do the same thing but use only a small amount of water. The idea is to let your child care for the plant, conduct an experiment that controls for different variables, and observe the differences.

Leaf collection   Age: 4 – 5
Science Skills: Classifying; comparing and contrasting
Directions: Collect ten to twelve different types of leaves from your neighborhood and sort by shape, color, and edge patterns. First allow your children to categorize the leaves however they want and then guide them to find other ways to sort the leaves. (This is especially fun during the fall season.)

As you complete these activities and experiments, sit alongside your child and actively engage in discussion. Ask questions, introduce age-appropriate concepts, and encourage reasoning. Pinterest has many other helpful ideas you can utilize, and they can be meaningful if you cultivate your child's ability to think scientifically while doing the activities.

Whether you search for additional ideas online, or simply endeavor to provide an early science education, keep the following standards in mind. They represent state and national goals in science for preschool children.

Science standards for preschool children

Birth – 12 months

During this age, parents should help children to:
- Use the five senses to explore their world.
- Observe science in life, pictures, and children's books.

12 – 24 months

Your children should begin to learn to:
- Identify the sun, moon, and stars.

- Use terms to identify position (e.g., in front of, behind, and inside).
- Identify hot and cold.
- Identify basic body parts.
- Describe how animals sometimes have different parts (e.g., tails, fins, trunks, and whiskers).

2 – 3 years old

Your children should begin to learn to:
- Recognize that sunlight keeps us warm.
- Identify types of weather and incorporate related terms (e.g., rainy, sunny, foggy, windy, cloudy, and stormy).
- Identify shadows from the sun or another light source.
- Distinguish between different bodies of water, including lakes, creeks, rivers, and oceans.
- Identify different types of objects on Earth (e.g., rocks, soil, trees, and sand).
- Identify properties of matter.
- Determine if objects will float or sink.
- Distinguish between push and pull.
- Explore and identify a variety of plants and animals.
- Identify offspring names such as deer & fawns and dogs & puppies.
- Describe how germs spread and explain prevention techniques.
- Summarize safety rules (e.g., look both ways before crossing the street, and don't run with a toothbrush in your mouth).

4 – 6 years old

Your children should begin to learn to:
- Identify different types of clouds.
- Explain the four seasons.
- Notice weather patterns over the course of a year; it changes day to day and seasonally.
- Discuss wind power.

- Talk about how weather differs depending on the region of the country.
- Observe and identify different states of water.
- Discuss uses of water.
- Discuss the importance of protecting our planet by reducing, reusing, and recycling.
- Compare different types of terrain (e.g., mountains, hills, plains, and deserts).
- Discover the effects of gravity and magnetism.
- Demonstrate mechanical forces such as teeter-totters and basic tools.
- Discuss life cycles of plants and animals.
- Identify the structures of plants (e.g., stems, roots, and leaves).
- Distinguish between living and non-living things.
- Explain how humans, plants, and animals all need air, food, and water to live and grow.
- Identify animal homes and habitats.
- Identify healthy foods for our bodies.

Experience science

Your children will learn best when they have multiple and varied experiences. Science skills and knowledge sometimes take months or years to develop, so be sure to regularly incorporate opportunities for preschoolers to make meaning. Use numerous resources to help. There are many online simulations, science apps, books, and television shows that can facilitate discovery.

Also improve school readiness by connecting science with other content areas. You will naturally expand a child's vocabulary when you teach science, but also work on math when conducting experiences and activities.

Young kids will learn scientific concepts if you foster a sense of excitement about the world. Take advantage of their inherent interest and use everyday items and experiences as a launching point. Explore, ask inquiry-based questions, be observant, and guide your child's understandings of scientific phenomena. Be intentional by looking for critters and birds in your own yard and by visiting a farm, fish hatchery, or wildlife sanctuary. Even visit a local sport store equipped with stuffed or mounted animals (such as Cabela's or Bass Pro Shop) to teach science. Turn what your child sees and does into learning opportunities.

4

Literacy: Laying the Foundation

Preparing your young child to be a reader doesn't require a degree in education, but it does involve some intentionality. I (Annie) remember when this first came clear to me. I was a student teacher in a second-grade classroom sitting in on a parent-teacher conference early in the school year. One family arrived with their son (who was in the class) as well as two younger siblings who sat off to the side during the meeting. As the conference started, one of the younger siblings—the family's four-year-old daughter—started to read to the youngest sibling.

The classroom teacher and I were both surprised to hear a four-year-old reading already. The mother assured us she had done no direct teaching. Instead, the daughter had simply been paying attention while her older brother was learning to read. Because the family valued growth and learning, all kids learned literacy skills and knowledge.

If you are a parent of a busy young family and feel like you can do no more than simply read to your children each night, rest assured that you are helping them to become readers. In other words, intentionality does not mean you necessarily need to add a whole list of activities to your already busy schedule. There are a variety of easy-to-incorporate activities you can do as part of your daily routine. With repeated exposure, you will equip your children to be successful readers while enhancing quality time together.

It's important to remember that learning to read is a developmental process that connects for children at different ages. Parents should not be worried about their preschooler developing later than others, and slow progress is not necessarily indicative of a deficiency. If you have multiple children, also be careful not to compare one sibling to another.

Routine experiences with various pre-reading skills will build on each other, and children will read when their brains have made all the connections necessary for mastery. While teaching a child to read may seem like an attainable goal in kindergarten, and might appear to be irrefutable evidence of learning, there is so much leading up to it that must be mastered.

Even if students leave kindergarten without being able to "decode," or sound out a word, their brains are gaining knowledge. Rest assured—if you build foundational knowledge, your child will successfully read in the early years of elementary school.

Vocabulary development

As you naturally bond with your new little addition to the family, your infant is already beginning to develop language abilities. By simply talking to your baby as she coos and babbles, you are introducing sounds that will later be blended into words. As you comment on what you see around you, or what you read in books, you will build her vocabulary. Make it a point to talk to your infant as often as possible and you will put her on the path to becoming a reader without even knowing it.

During the toddler months, use pictures to help your kids come to understand the meaning of words. As you read books, ask if they know what some of the words mean. Then improve their knowledge of terms by asking questions that require descriptive language and detail, such as, "What is she wearing?" "What objects are on the page?" "How would you describe the animal you see in the picture?" "Which tree is the biggest?" "How can you tell?"

Challenge your toddler to use as many words as possible when he offers an answer. If he has difficulties stringing longer sentences together, ask additional prompting questions or provide your own detailed answer. If you do this frequently you will foster a sense of curiosity with new words, and your children will begin to ask their own who, what, where, when, why, and how questions.

Children logically want to make sense of the world and derive meaning on which to build. For the first few years of your little ones' lives, intentional and interactive play will be their classroom. These experiences are providing the foundation for vocabulary acquisition and oral communication. By age four or five, your inquisitive children may be asking you more and more about letters and sounds. They may be able to recognize the letters of their name in books or on signs as you drive around town.

You will continue to grow your preschooler's vocabulary by connecting words with everyday experiences. If you are at a park, talk about terms related to trees, birds, or man-made structures. While watching television or scrolling through a social media page, use expressive language and numerous adjectives to describe something you read, see, or hear.

Strive to grow your child's vocabulary by defining a new word every day. When possible, connect the new word with things he or she has already learned about. For example, a four-year-old likely understands many terms related to weather, such as rain, clouds, and sun. So the next time you discuss the weather, add a new word like thunder or condensation. Provide a definition, an analogy or simile, and an example to solidify understanding of the new term.

As your children listen to everyday conversations, they will automatically learn new vocabulary. Therefore, be sure to use normal language when speaking. While it is cute and fun to use "kiddy language," expand knowledge by including more complicated language. Kids are good listeners and will try to replicate the words they hear from adults. Besides, it is fun to hear a three-year-old trying to say "phenomenal."

Through daily discussion, preschoolers will begin to use many conventions of the English language. They will increasingly include suffixes, prefixes, prepositions, and plural forms of words in everyday language. They will get many words wrong (throwed instead of threw, deers instead of deer, telled versus told), so patiently and persistently take the time to make corrections. Stress that most past tense words end with –ed, and most plural animals end with –s, but talk about how we sometimes use different forms of words.

Parents can also develop a preschooler's vocabulary by making connections and by exploring word relationships. If your toddler sees a pair of scissors, describe its physical characteristics and demonstrate how people use them to cut things. Compare it with a knife, which is also used to cut things. Whenever you introduce a new word, include this type of detail along with the definition. After your child develops a bit of a vocabulary, then explore word relationships by:

- **Pointing out opposites.** Including opposites such as tall/short, good/bad, up/down, inside/outside, over/under, open/closed, and light/dark. Get to a point where you state a word and your child has to come up with the opposite.
- **Incorporating words with similar meanings.** For instance, when people jog, run, and sprint, they are all moving fast.
- **Exploring how words sometimes have multiple meanings.** They might hear a dog bark, but there is also bark on a tree.
- **Categorizing words based on characteristics.** Apples, pizza, and bread can be grouped together since they are all foods. Dogs, cats, and squirrels can all go in the animal category.

- **Discussing how some words relate to each other.** A tricycle has three wheels and a triangle has three sides.

It is important to note that learning to differentiate between letters and numbers requires repeated experiences and correction. At first, toddlers won't understand reading and counting because they won't yet have enough experience to make sense of each symbol. When you count objects, remind your children how numbers are used to count. As you read books, explain how letters make words and you are reading the words to tell a story.

Be encouraging and foster inquisitive little minds—they are learning so much. As children assign meaning to words, vocabulary acquisition and higher-order conversations will naturally flow.

Oral communication

As one's vocabulary increases, so does the ability to communicate orally. We have stressed the importance of talking with your children throughout this book. There is yet another reason why we do so. When you regularly speak about familiar people, things, places, events, and experiences with kids, their oral communication skills will improve. In addition, a large part of communication often consists of body language, facial expressions, gestures, and tone of voice. Therefore, it is important to teach children to:

- **Use nonverbal forms of communication to express words, feelings, and thoughts.** Smile when you are happy. Shrug to say you don't care. Point to show your choice.
- **Express meaning with inflection, volume, and speed.** For example, when we are really excited about something, we might speak loudly and more quickly, with animated gestures.

- **Tell stories with different inflections and cadences.**
- **Identify emotions in pictures.** Does the person in the book look happy? Sad? Excited?
- **Use objects to represent ideas.** For instance, kids might use paper scraps to represent water. Our daughter once wanted to float a toy boat on a pretend "lake."
- **Follow directions.** It is often helpful to ask your little one to restate directions.
- **Listen intently.** Children should stop what they are doing, maintain good eye contact, and acknowledge that they listened with some sort of response.
- **Draw pictures to represent things.**

There are many things caregivers can do to teach essential communication skills. As usual, it begins with modeling them. If your child is speaking to you, give him your complete attention. Let him finish his thoughts before you interrupt with your own. Show him you understand what he is saying by periodically nodding your head or by giving him verbal cues. Model what it looks like to take turns during a conversation with multiple exchanges.

When your toddler speaks with you, encourage her to use complete sentences. If she is unable, restate her thought with a complete sentence so she begins to learn what longer sentences sound like. Encourage her to initiate conversations. Have her make up stories related to a recent experience, prompt her to tell a family member about an event from last week, and encourage questions. When your preschoolers regularly engage in conversations with adults, other children, siblings, and community members, you will foster an increased attention span and improve oral communication.

Read to your child every day!

As we've said before, you play a unique and crucial role in building reading readiness. Reading to your child each day is one of the most effective things you can do. The amount of learning that takes place while your little one sits cuddled in your lap in the afternoon, or before bed, is remarkable. Before she is even aware of what is happening, you are teaching her how to hold a book and turn the pages correctly. You are communicating information about written symbols and story structure.

Learning to read is a continuum. You build knowledge every time you read to and interact with your little one. Every experience and every conversation moves him closer to becoming a reader. Even preschoolers who memorize a simple book that states "I see a tree, I see a book, I see a heart," where the pictures match the words on each page, is engaging in valuable pre-reading skills. They are recognizing how letters and words have meaning, and how pictures can provide clues. When a child can point to each word as she "reads," she also learns basic conventions of literature: Print moves from left to right, there are spaces between words, and paragraphs flow from top to bottom.

Now that you understand how much is happening while you engage your child in conversation and reading, you might wonder where to begin. Books with one word and a matching picture are a great place to start. As you teach your child what a cat looks like and point to the word cat, her brain is making the connection to be drawn upon later when she is ready to read. These types of books not only introduce language to your infant, but they can also be used later with your toddler and preschooler to match pictures with words.

Books with repetitive or predictive text are a good next step. As your child becomes familiar with a book, you can leave out words and have her fill in the correct word. Board books like *From Head to Toe* by Eric Carle, and *Brown Bear, Brown Bear, What Do You See?* by Bill Martin Jr. and Eric Carle, are examples of quality books with repetitive text and whimsical pictures.

We were able to obtain an assortment of board and plastic books as gifts, and we are convinced that our daughter's love of literature was formed at an early age as a result. While books become chew toys more often than not during infancy, the textured pages, squeaky sounds, and bright colors build interest in reading.

Letter names and sounds

Exposure to letters can easily start with ABC books, puzzles, and magnetic letters. Our daughter loved to be read to, and it was natural that much of her knowledge of letters and their sounds first came from reading alphabet books together with us. As she was learning words we would ask her to point to the ball, baby, or bat while saying the words, making the /b/ sound, and then pointing to the letter B on the page (/ / represents the letter sound not the letter name).

As a toddler continually hears these words she will begin to hear and start to distinguish the beginning sounds. When you ask if she can think of another word that begins with /b/, you are making her draw on previous connections. You are laying the foundation for the ability to engage orally with language later in school.

The toy company Melissa & Doug makes fantastic educational puzzles. A particular favorite in our house was the ABC puzzle that says the letter and an associated word. Another well-loved toy for us was the LeapFrog Fridge Phonics Magnetic Letter Set. As we did the dishes or made dinner, our daughter would put letters into the bus and hear the letter name as well as the sound each one makes.

As kids learn to identify the letters with these tools, it is a great opportunity to see if they can pronounce each letter sound. Begin with the hard consonant sounds only (for instance, with the letter G, use the sound it makes in "great" and do not initially introduce the soft sound as in "gem") and use the most common vowel sounds as in the following.

A: Apple
E: Egg

I: Igloo
O: Octopus
U: Umbrella

Introduce letters in a personal way by using your child's name. Our daughter's name hung in uppercase letters over her bed when she was a toddler. It was natural to regularly talk about each letter, and we explained how those letters together form her name. She was able to recognize and spell her name before she knew any other letters.

During the toddler years, help your children develop the ability to recognize uppercase letters and say the associated sounds. Then, during ages 4 – 6 you can slowly introduce the soft sounds of consonants, the other vowel sounds, and lowercase letters. Here are some more ways you can teach the letters of the alphabet.

- Letter matching game: Cut 3 x 5 cards in half and write the same letter on each of the two halves (use uppercase letters to start). Make a set of the entire alphabet and ask your child to find the matches. Start with just a few letters such as the letters in your child's name.

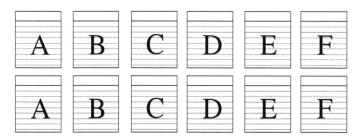

- Spell your child's name with magnetic letters or with the 3 x 5 cards from the activity above.
- Play "I spy" while driving in the car. Ask your children to look for letters: "I spy with my little eye the letter M."
- ABC bingo game: Create 4 x 4 bingo boards with sixteen varying letters printed in each square (again, start

with uppercase letters). Use 3 x 5 cards and print a single letter on each card, thus creating 26 cards. Put the cards face down and then begin the game by turning them over one at a time. If your bingo board has the letter, cross it off. Keep turning over cards until someone has four in a row. While playing, see if your child can say the letters and sounds they make. If he or she is unable to produce the letter name and sound say, "this is an S, it makes a /s/ sound."

ABC BINGO			
B	S	U	Q
P	F	M	W
I	V	Z	O
E	R	K	D

ABC BINGO			
T	A	H	C
D	X	L	J
I	G	E	N
Y	S	P	U

Once your child is familiar with most of the letter sounds, then incorporate the following activities.

- Alphabet match up: Buy or create a set of letters and matching pictures (e.g., the letter C and a picture of a cat). Mix them up and then match the letter and the picture that begins with the same sound.

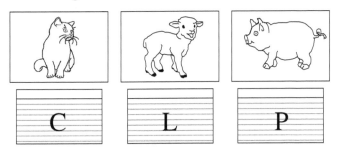

- Play guessing games in the car or while waiting in line at the grocery store. What animals start with the /a/

sound? Or, I spy something that begins with the /t/ sound.

- Make your own ABC book using construction paper and pictures. Find a bunch of pictures in a magazine (or print them from the Internet) beginning with each letter sound. Use uppercase letters and glue the corresponding pictures onto the construction paper. Then bind all the pages with staples or string.

Phonemic awareness

Phonemic awareness may be a new term to you. It is basically the understanding that words are made of individual sounds (or phonemes). Children are on the way to becoming successful readers when they are able to take notice of, distinguish, and manipulate isolated sounds within a spoken word.

This skill is highlighted and built upon in kindergarten and first grade, but there are other skills that can be introduced and developed prior to kindergarten. In particular, parents will lay a foundation if they regularly introduce rhyming words, alliteration, sentence segmentation, syllables, and onsets and rimes (in the word cat, "c–" is the onset and "–at" is the rime).

Read poetry and nursery rhymes to introduce your little ones to the practice of listening to isolated sounds within words while exploring word relationships. Listen to songs such as "Down by the Bay" (popularly sung by children's music artist Raffi) as an entertaining way to train the brain to hear rhyming sounds.

Once familiar with the song, make up your own silly rhyming words: Have you ever seen a frog riding on a hog? Have you ever seen a duck driving a truck? Our four-year-old was not able to produce many of her own rhymes at that age, but she sure giggled when Mommy and Daddy came up with silly ones. When she was a little younger, at around age three, she was able to complete a rhyming puzzle. It had numerous pieces with pictures and words and she had to match pairs such as block/sock, rake/cake, and tree/bee.

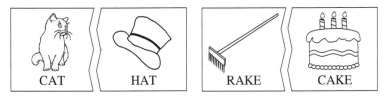

CAT   HAT   RAKE   CAKE

When discussing rhyming words, explain how words with the same ending sound are part of the same word family. If cat and bat rhyme, what other words are part of the "–at" family? Can your preschooler think of others such at hat, fat, sat, mat, and rat? As you play with these rhyming words you can begin to segment the words into beginning and ending sounds to introduce onset (beginning sound) and rime (the first vowel and consonant cluster after it).

Talk about how /h/ and /at/ says "hat" or /f/ and /at/ says "fat." Your child may not initially be able to blend the sounds together to say the words, but these activities will build phonemic awareness. The more often you identify rhyming words and listen to songs, the more language connections your child's brain will make.

Counting or clapping words in a sentence demonstrates an additional ability to segment sounds and words. For instance, while going for a walk say to your child, "I see a bird. Let's count the number of words in that sentence. As I say each word let's hold up a finger." Say the sentence again slowly, putting up a finger for each word. Then count to see how many total words are in the sentence. Try this with different, short sentences with varying numbers of words.

It is also important for children to hear and distinguish syllables within a word. Splitting and combining compound words such as "cowboy," "upstairs," and "baseball" is a good place to start. It allows them to hear and manipulate syllables. Say to your child, "two words together 'cow' (hold out right hand) and 'boy' (hold out left hand) make one word 'cowboy' (clap hands together). Let's say it together, holding out each hand and then clap when we say the compound word." By adding in the hand gestures you are attaching a kinesthetic connection for the brain and helping your kids to understand how two words combined sometimes make one word.

Another way to develop phonemic awareness is through alliterative word play. Make up silly sentences or stories where many words start with the same beginning sound. A well known example is "Peter Piper picked a peck of pickled peppers." Emphasize the repeated sound and ask your child what sound she hears. Start with beginning sounds that are easy to draw out and enunciate, such as /m/, /s/, and /f/. (When first trying this activity with four-year-olds, they are able to hear the /m/ sound and /s/ sound easier than /g/ or /k/ sounds.)

Initially your child may not be able to isolate the sound, but keep playing and eventually it will click. Look for other picture books at your library that use alliteration, rhythm, and rhyming. Dr. Seuss has a series of excellent books for playing with these types of sounds.

Writing

Before children learn to write they must first develop fine motor skills, which include hand strength, dexterity, and coordination. Parents can help increase these skills by offering many opportunities for intentional play with specific fine motor activities. Some ways to develop these skills include:[1]

- Stringing buttons or beads on pipe cleaners.
- Picking up items with oversized tweezers or tongs.
- Stacking fruit loops on raw spaghetti noodles.
- Making shapes out of marshmallows and toothpicks.
- Cutting colored straws in pieces and stacking them on pipe cleaners.
- Matching and hanging socks on a line with clothespins.

When you introduce your young children to new activities, simply provide the materials and see what happens. Initially let them explore and create without direction or promptings. Remember, a lot of learning happens with just personal exploration. When they begin to show signs of boredom or frustration, then offer guidance to help make fun patterns or follow specific directions.

Incorporate these types of tasks as young as your children are able, usually between six months and a year old. With practice, they will gradually improve their ability to grasp and control items with skill and precision. Around age three or four, toddlers with strong hand and shoulder muscles—as well as the core muscles needed to sit up straight—are usually ready to learn how to properly hold a pencil.

It is important to learn the correct form as it is difficult to retrain children with improper pencil grips. When first teaching, use a shorter pencil—toddlers are more likely to hold it correctly. It might also be helpful to use larger diameter pencils. Use a thick golf pencil or break one in half and show how to pinch the pencil with the thumb and index finger while it rests on the middle finger. The non-pointed end of the writing utensil should naturally fall between the base of the thumb and index finger. If it is a struggle to grasp with just the three fingers, then hold a cotton ball with the ring finger and pinky to force using only the other three.[2]

Model proper writing form, guide little fingers onto the pencil, and then let them scribble and draw pretend pictures to their heart's content. With encouragement and direction, scribbles will turn into rudimentary pictures, shapes, objects, and other intentional drawings. Use a wide variety of writing tools—including chalk, crayons, and colored pencils—and teach your child to trace basic shapes such as lines, triangles, squares, and circles. With practice, he will eventually be able to draw shapes and pictures without help. As your preschooler completes pictures and drawings, ask him to describe his creation. He will often express quite a bit more than what is seen in the picture.

The next step includes writing the letters of the alphabet. However, wait to practice writing until your child has developed the fine motor skills to properly hold a pencil. Use only uppercase letters initially and begin by asking your child to print the letters of her own name. If necessary, use stencils, trace over existing letters, and provide instruction to support learning.

As she practices writing her own name, explain how we write letters of words from left to right. Once your preschooler is capable of writing the uppercase letters, then slowly introduce the lowercase letters. If you provide regular opportunities for practice, your child's letters will look more and more refined each time.

To help with this process, you can use multiple tactile modes such as tracing letters in sand or a salt tray. Also make letters out of Play-Doh, Wikki Stix, or pipe cleaners. As with this activity, or any other activity we include in the book, strive to create a no-pressure environment. If your child loses interest, simply move on to something else and come back to tracing letters again later.

Reading comprehension

Writing and reading go hand in hand when building literacy skills. Readers get better at spelling, punctuation, and writing mechanics, while writers learn how to read literature more fluently.[3] This leads to our final component of literacy, which includes your child's ability to understand the meaning of literature. While most children may not develop the ability to read until they are in kindergarten or first grade, they can process the stories and events in books as you read to them.

They can make conclusions and draw from prior knowledge and experience to make sense of the stories.

As you read alongside your toddler and preschooler, ask about what is happening in the story. Discuss the characters and setting. Frequently reference the pictures in the book and relate them to the book's storyline. See if your kids understand what you are reading and what is happening in the story by asking questions, such as: "What do you think will happen next?" "Can you summarize what just happened?" "What do you think of a certain character in the story?" "What letters do you see on this page and in this word?" "How is an event in the story the same or different from another part of the book or from a different story?"

These types of inquiries will require your children to be active participants and will develop many valuable reading comprehension skills. You will be teaching them to:

- Draw information from pictures and explain the meaning of illustrations.
- Make connections among the characters of the book.
- Identify specific details in a story.
- Inquire about unknown words in the text.
- Ask questions about the storyline or a character.
- Recognize common signs and symbols, such as a stop sign or a symbol for a public bathroom.
- Identify the main topic or major events in literature.

All of these skills translate to another important comprehension strategy—the ability to pretend read. When toddlers pretend read, they are often summarizing a story, making meaning of pictures, and creating details of a character or setting. It is such a joy to watch a young boy or girl sit alone, open up a book, and verbally make up a story while looking at picture illustrations or by recalling details from when Dad read the book earlier.

To enhance your children's abilities in this area, be sure to include a variety of age-appropriate forms of literature. Read fictional story books, non-fictional science and history texts, poems, counting books, and plays. Read stories from different eras and cultures, then discuss how the stories are similar or different from your child's everyday life. Lastly, make it a point to re-read stories often. Kids will be able to pick out additional details and better comprehend what is written as you read a book for the third, tenth, or fiftieth time.

Literacy standards for preschool children

Birth – 12 months

During this age, parents should:
- Read many books to their babies every day.
- Regularly communicate (verbal and nonverbal) with their babies.
- Share stories.

12 – 24 months

Your children should begin to learn to:
- Identify basic objects and animals in a book.
- Identify the meaning of words by looking at pictures.

2 – 3 years old

Your children should begin to learn to:
- Recognize uppercase letters in their own name.
- Pronounce the first letter of their own name.
- Recognize words that rhyme.
- Differentiate between letters and numbers.
- Spell and write their own name.
- Pretend read.
- Recognize the basic features and organization of print (e.g., we read from left to right, top to bottom, and page by page; the title is on the cover of books; certain sequences of letters make words, and words have spaces in between them).

- Provide detailed descriptions of pictures and events.
- Print uppercase letters of their own name.
- Identify emotions in pictures.
- Ask and answer questions related to visual texts.

4 – 6 years old

Your children should begin to learn to:
- Identify and name uppercase and lowercase letters of the alphabet.
- Trace letters or create them out of Play-Doh.
- Print uppercase and lowercase letters.
- Pronounce the sounds of all 26 letters.
- Speak and read with inflection and cadence.
- Recognize alliteration.
- Write from left to right and top to bottom.
- Write letters to form words.
- Use increasingly complex words in conversations.
- Identify words with multiple meanings.
- Identify characters, settings, and main themes of stories.
- Use tone, gestures, nonverbal communication, and facial expressions to express words and thoughts.
- Use volume, tone, and speed to express meaning.
- Make up their own stories.
- Match words that rhyme.
- Pretend read with greater detail.
- Summarize stories and events in books.
- Retell stories.
- Predict what might happen in children's stories.
- Explain meaning of and identify information from pictures and illustrations.
- Pronounce isolated sounds in words.
- State the letter when they hear most consonant and short vowel sounds.
- Demonstrate one-to-one letter/sound correspondence (e.g., each letter of the word CAT makes a specific sound).

- Spell simple words phonetically using their knowledge of sound-letter relationships.
- Connect words with pictures (with support).

Create a language-rich environment

Children who do not develop early literacy skills—especially phonemic awareness, alphabet knowledge, and vocabulary acquisition—prior to kindergarten are at risk for reading difficulties later on. And it can be difficult to overcome literacy deficiencies. Most students who are low performing readers in first grade are poor readers in fourth grade, as well.[4]

So as soon as your child is born, create a culture that values language development. Interact with your newborn. Regularly communicate with your toddler and preschooler. Ask questions, read and share fun stories, encourage discussion, display letters and words around your home, and play literacy-related games.

Read, converse, and interact with your young kids and they will absorb and learn so much. Written and verbal words are a natural part of your home's culture—just be sure to intentionally grow your children's skills.[5] Do a play-by-play of your day's activities to teach vocabulary words. Include a variety of new terms and don't be afraid to incorporate larger words.

Our daughter would sometimes use "binoculars" and "generous" in sentences when she was three years old. It wasn't because she was advanced or gifted. It was simply because we made it a point to include such terms while talking with her. Spend a lot of time at your local library—even libraries in the smallest of towns often have many great resources parents can tap into. Don't be overwhelmed, intimidated, or pressured by the role you play. Instead, embrace it and enjoy watching your kids grow.

5

Social Studies: Understanding Culture & Society

If you were to conduct an Internet search asking how people would describe society today, you would get a variety of interesting responses. Unfortunately, in our increasingly divisive culture, many of them are negative. People use adjectives such as chaotic, angry, tense, thoughtless, and uncompromising. With so much discord in America today, perhaps we should all remember the importance of cultivating a strong educational foundation in social studies.

The National Council for the Social Studies (NCSS), an organization devoted to supporting teachers and parents in this area, details numerous aspects of human society that preschool children should learn, including:

1. How to effectively work with others in a culturally diverse society.
2. The authority structures and role of government.
3. A person's civic duties.
4. Basic economic principles and how we make, share, and consume goods.
5. An understanding of historical events.
6. The varying geographies and environments in our world.[1]

In essence, the goal of a social studies education is to learn skills and concepts that will help children become informed, engaged, and responsible citizens.[2] Perhaps if we all helped our children develop these key understandings, we would begin to use more positive adjectives to describe our culture today.

When we teach toddlers and preschoolers social studies, we are also nurturing a sense of self and helping them to better understand the world.[3] During infancy, learning begins as babies explore their own bodies and immediate surroundings. It continues during toddlerhood as kids acquire knowledge about family, community structures, and their place in society.

Just about all people live in some sort of community defined by countless cultural elements (food, clothing, technology, celebrations, education, politics, race, hobbies, value systems, ethnicity, language, religion, gender roles, and traditions to name some). Parents must provide early educational experiences to help young children negotiate the many complex social elements.

While some of these topics seem too abstract for preschoolers, parents are in fact able to teach these ideas in concrete ways.[4] Young children are developmentally able to begin learning fundamental ideas about social diversity, government, economics, history, and geography. Caregivers simply need to connect each topic with preschool experiences and activities.

At age one, babies begin to notice differences and similarities of people within their immediate surroundings. As toddlers, they become aware of race and gender differences and notice how others might speak, dress, or behave differently.[5] When between the ages of four and six years old, children are able to sequentially order historical events in their own lives.[6]

Keep reading because we include many more tangible, specific ideas for each of the five main subtopics within social studies (social diversity, government, economics, history, and geography).

Social diversity

In social studies, educators emphasize the significance of a person's ability to relate well with others in a diverse society. Before preschoolers can appreciate diversity, however, they must first comprehend their own characteristics and those of their immediate family. What types of food do you like to eat? What types of clothes do you wear? What do you value? What is your family heritage? What traditions do you appreciate? What is your belief system? What are your hobbies and interests?

Identify and talk about elements of your culture. Then as you interact with people in society, your preschooler will learn about human diversity as you examine similarities and differences between other people's characteristics and your own.

Foster a sense of appreciation and pride with your family, but also avoid negative comparisons. There isn't anything wrong with a friend who likes to eat something your family prefers not to consume. If someone lives in an urban area, they shouldn't pass judgment on a rural family who likes to hunt. On the other hand, rural residents should avoid speaking negatively of city living.

As adults, we must be careful with our own verbal and nonverbal messages because children are very observant and will notice how we respond to differing interests, values, norms, and actions. Our response to a situation might indicate to children that some individuals hold a lesser status than others.[7] Alternatively, a positive response of respect will teach little ones how to thrive in diverse settings.

One powerful way to nurture a respect for differences is through children's literature. The Walt Disney Company produced a series of books as part of their Small World Library. Each volume has a couple of Disney characters traveling to a country and experiencing a different culture. At the conclusion of each book, they include information about the country and then declare, "Each country has many different customs and places that make it special."[8] When we read about and discuss this type of mindset, children will develop a genuine interest in the lives and customs of diverse people groups.

Parents can do this with any book that includes human diversity, or by simply telling stories of others. Tell the story of the life of a farmer or a mechanic or a city worker. Talk about life on a Native American reservation or traditions of someone who lives in a different country. Teach your preschooler about other people's customs and daily routines.

We can all help children embrace diversity by showing artwork, looking at pictures, and listening to music from different cultures. Make connections with your child's experiences to help make differences more concrete. For example, just as many Chinese people like to eat egg custard tarts for dessert, some Americans enjoy apple pie with ice cream.

Early exposure to the needs of others is vital in a society where people are often consumed with only their own thoughts and desires. It truly is a blessing to serve those in our community and beyond. Therefore, we should model how to share our time, money, and resources. When parents and caregivers encourage preschoolers to share, care for a friend, use respectful language, and value diversity, they will promote fairness and equity for all.[9]

Government and civics

Many would argue that one purpose of government is to ensure that all people have an equal opportunity to freely pursue their dreams and exercise their rights. Government leaders create and enforce laws to protect us, and the rules you establish in your home are a microcosm of that authority. When you explain to your little one how rules are usually created to help everyone, you will prepare her to function in a school setting and a democratic society.

Kids need to learn that there are consequences when we don't follow rules. There are often immediate consequences because the child isn't obeying the parent, but an equally important lesson to introduce is how rule breakers can produce general disorder and unsafe conditions. A children's book entitled, *What if Everybody Did That?* helps illustrate this idea. On one page, the book shows a child running in the grocery store. On the next page, it shows a picture where everybody is running in the store with images of chaos as people are bumping into each other and knocking stuff over.[10] What a creative way to teach children why we have rules.

Teach the importance of following rules and then associate family guidelines with government authority to develop this key understanding. Also point out how different organizations might have different rules. Day care centers, libraries, churches, and other households might have a whole unique set of expectations as compared to your own. For instance, while it might be okay to wear shoes in your home, your friend's household may not allow it. Foster your child's ability to adapt to the differences. Sometimes we have to alter our desires or preferences, and we learn to sacrifice out of respect and for the good of the whole community.

Another aspect of an effective government includes the importance of carrying out our civic duties. Parents can have a positive impact if they expose young children to lessons related to community membership. Start with your family and discuss what it means to be a good "citizen" within your home. Teach your children to work with family members and be helpers with daily household tasks.

Help them to recognize that we often have roles and responsibilities both inside and outside of our home. Whether in a classroom, in the neighborhood, or at a public event, kids can learn to serve the community and value the norms of the culture.

Economics: Money and work

Part of each person's contribution to society includes wise money management and service to the community through work. For that reason, it is important to have conversations about different types of jobs and how each can help society. Whether people are plumbers, garbage removal providers, doctors, teachers, or firefighters, they all play an important role.

Some occupations are too difficult for young children to understand, so start with the ones they see or experience. If an electrician comes to your home to fix a light, if you deposit a check with a bank teller, or if you get pulled over by a police officer with your child in the car, take time to describe what each worker does and how they serve us. Also tell work related stories, encourage questions, and ask if it might be fun to have certain jobs.

Workplace labor naturally leads to another important lesson parents can teach preschoolers; namely, how to manage money. Work and money are often intertwined. Explain how people work for money to buy things they need (food and clothes) and want (toys and treats). Examine the many cause-and-effect relationships with young learners to further teach these important concepts.

- **If you** give money to a store clerk, **then you will** receive something in return.

  Preschool example: Create a pretend store in your living room and use fake money or coins to purchase items. You can also practice counting with money.

- **If you** work hard to complete a task, **then you will** feel a sense of pride and accomplishment.

  Preschool example: After completing a craft or a piece of artwork that took some time to complete, ask your preschooler what he thinks of the finished product. (Kids are usually very proud of their creations.)

- **If you** work hard to complete a task, **then you will** earn money or receive some kind of reward or incentive.

Preschool example: When your young child helps rake the leaves in autumn, reward her with a special treat at the local ice cream store.

- **If you** save money, **then you will** have it when you really want or need it for something.

Preschool example: Tell your child that every time she completes a task outside of her usual chores she will receive a token. Once she receives ten tokens, go to the store and buy a special toy.

- **If you** work together, **then you will** be more productive and have more fun.

Preschool example: Point out how your child was able to build a bigger fort when working with a friend.

- **If you** have limited resources, **then you will** have to decide between two choices.

Preschool example: While at a toy store, tell your child you only have enough money to purchase one toy.

- **If you** work on something you are good at, **then you will** enjoy the work.

Preschool example: Identify your child's strengths, such as hopping on one leg for a long time, drawing good faces with colored pencils, or putting something together with blocks, and then discuss her joyous emotions.

Unfortunately, many adults have not learned some of the lessons related to work and money, so it is important to begin to instill them when your children are four to six years old. You can further teach about money by involving your preschoolers when buying items at the store. Show the different types of bills and coins while completing a transaction. Identify the different images, names, and values of currency.

Finally, and perhaps most importantly, teach the difference between a want and a need. As any parent knows, if you walk through the toy section or candy aisle of a store with toddlers, they will make their desires known. But kids must learn they can't always get everything they want. They must be taught the difference between truly needing something and just wanting something.

History

Perhaps the most common facet of social studies in school is the knowledge and understanding of past events. Preschoolers can begin to comprehend the concept of history by recalling past experiences in their own lives. The best way to think about your child's personal story is to look at your family's pictures. And as you view images, help her to recognize how things change over time. For instance, in a picture of her as an infant, she had very little hair. As a two-year-old, her hair was longer. Now, as a four-year-old, her hair is so long you can put it in a pony tail.

Teach your child to distinguish between something that happened in the past versus events happening now or might happen in the future. To accomplish this, simply use language such as:

Past events:	"When you were…"
	"The last time we…"
	"You already…"
Current events:	"Now we are…"
	"You are currently…"
	"We are on our way to…"
Future events:	"Next time we will…"
	"Tomorrow, we are going to…"
	"I can't wait until…"

History also involves learning about major historical figures and events in society. Therefore, tell stories about your child's grandparents and great grandparents to expose him to traditions and experiences from a different time period. If you are visiting Grandma and Grandpa on vacation, ask what they did for fun as kids. Include influential events and well-known people who lived during the previous era.

If you are thin on family narratives, then read numerous children's books as a way to discuss historical information. As you read with your child, distinguish between something that recently occurred versus something that happened a long time ago. The goal at this age isn't necessarily to get your preschoolers to remember historical facts. Instead, the goal is to help them develop a sense of time, which is an important precursor to later success in social studies.

Geography

Caregivers will empower children to better achieve in social studies when they introduce lessons related to location, distance, direction, and the basic elements of a map. As with so many other topics, start with your child's experiences. If she has been in the mountains, in an urban setting, in the plain states, along an ocean, or to any other geographic location, talk about the environment. Discuss topics such as landscape, population density, and how location influences climate and weather.

We live in a rural setting in the Great Lakes region, so we mention hills, lakes, and the lack of stop lights. Family friends live near a popular beach destination in the south, so they are able to point out the palm trees, sand dunes, and how it is always busy with many cars and people. Introduce various man made and natural features in your own neighborhood, and then compare your setting with relatives and friends who live in different parts of the country.

Preschool geography is also about developing a sense of direction and place. As toddlers, they should learn the name of the street, town, and state in which you live. See if they can recognize your neighborhood when you return home from a car trip. Teach the specific numbers and letters of your home address as a way to reinforce math and literacy.

Take a walk or drive through other neighborhoods and point out various street or town names to illustrate how different areas have different identifiers. While you are doing all of this, introduce key words such as up, down, forward, backwards, sideways, left, and right. Strive to get to a point where your child will follow directions when prompted to move in a certain direction.

A final objective in geography is to recognize a map and identify some of the basic elements included on one. Explain how maps tell us where places are located. Point out the green forests, the lined roadways, the blue bodies of water, the contoured mountains, and the cities represented by small circles. If you show a state or county map to your child, he will likely ask about so many other symbols and colors, too.

The first activity in the next section is a great way to teach your children about this. A handful of other activities are included to get you thinking about different ways you can expose your preschoolers to many of the subtopics within social studies.

Social studies activities

Create a map   Age: 4 − 6

Subtopic: Geography; location
Directions: Draw a picture or use blocks, sand, or any other materials and create a two- or three-dimensional map with your child. Create representations of topographical features such as hills, forests, houses, or farmland. As you complete the map, use many vocabulary words related to location and features generally seen on maps. Allow your children to freely

create and use their imagination. You could also create a basic map of your own backyard or neighborhood.

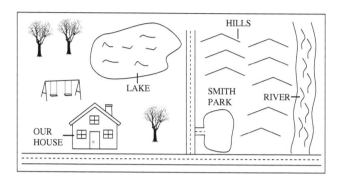

Compare & contrast   Age: 4 – 6
Subtopic: Cultural diversity
Directions: Using the Internet or magazines, find three or four pictures of people from different cultures. Take two at a time and ask your little one what he sees in each picture. If he isn't sure what to say, ask him questions such as: "What do you notice about their clothes?" "What foods do you see?" "What about their skin color?" "What does it look like they are doing in the picture?" Once you have a complete description of both pictures, then talk about the similarities and differences between the two. Remember, stress to your child how culture isn't only about skin color, race, or ethnicity. It also includes socioeconomic status, religion, rural or urban settings, education, geographic identity, age, language, family traditions, interests, worldviews, the arts, media, technology, and so much more.

Simon Says   Age: 4 – 6
Subtopic: Direction; location
Directions: We all know the popular game Simon Says. Use it to help your child get a better sense of direction: Simon says, "Move two steps forward." "Spin to your left." This activity also helps with motor development.

Treasure map Age: 4 – 6

Subtopic: Geography; location

Directions: In this activity, a parent creates a basic map of your home, yard, or local park. Start at a designated spot and place an X where the treasure is located. (You can use a piece of candy or small toy for the treasure.) Before your child searches for the treasure with you, discuss the features indicated on your map and the different routes you might take to get to the X. While on the hunt, provide assistance if your child gets stuck.

Sequential timeline Age: 4 – 6

Subtopic: History

Directions: Print three or four pictures of major events or experiences from your child's life and see if she can order them sequentially. You might include a picture of her as an infant, a picture of when she first started crawling, and one from a friend's birthday party you recently attended. The idea isn't to trick her or make it difficult to order, but to help her remember past events. This will also foster an understanding of language that distinguishes between events that happened a long time ago versus more recent events.

Play store Age: 4 – 6

Subtopic: Economics

Directions: Use coins or play money and create a pretend cash register (while unnecessary, you could also purchase an inexpensive one at a toy store). Then set up a series of toys, dolls, candy, and other items you might want to include in your "store." Create price tags for each item and then let your child purchase items. The intent is to practice counting, model the idea that we exchange money for things, and teach that some items cost more than others.

Mini society simulation   Age: 4 – 6

Subtopic: Government

Directions: Use your living room as a city, dolls as citizens, and props for buildings to simulate life in your mini society. Designate a doll to be the leader of the city who will then create rules and laws that all the other characters must follow. Pretend there is a park to play in, a school for children to attend, a store to buy things, police officers to help others, and include any other fun components of society. Let your child be imaginative with different character roles, and proactively engage in conversations about the responsibility and purposes of government.

Here's another variation of this idea. Invite some other parents with children over and help the kids set up a play area as a city with different stores, schools, and other community buildings. Each child might take turns acting out a different role, such as a store keeper, a librarian, or a bus driver. Once you get your preschoolers started, they usually take off with their own ideas. Be sure to share ideas and knowledge about communities and businesses during this activity.

Social studies standards for preschool children

12 – 24 months

Your children should begin to learn to:
- Notice differences and similarities in their own environment.
- Identify basic personal characteristics (e.g., brown hair, dark skin, green eyes, a big smile, and long legs).

2 – 3 years old

Your children should begin to learn to:
- Identify characteristics of your home and other familiar places.
- Develop an increased awareness of differences among people (e.g., race, gender, behaviors, and customs).
- Work together to achieve a common goal.
- Express needs and desires without whining.
- Work independently.
- Understand and follow rules.
- Understand consequences when violating rules.
- Use coins to practice counting.
- Identify locations in your home (e.g., living room, bedroom, and kitchen).
- Name letters and numbers in your home address.
- Recognize their own neighborhood and describe immediate surroundings.
- Describe different modes of transportation.
- Identify and describe topographical features (e.g., mountains, lakes, and forests).

4 – 6 years old

Your children should begin to learn to:
- Reference past events.
- Retell a series of three or four events in proper order.
- Recognize change over time.
- Tell historical stories.
- Discuss cultural differences through literature and experiences.
- Differentiate between past, present, and future.
- Share information about their own family practices (e.g., traditions, food preferences, and hobbies).
- Take pride in accomplishments.
- Adjust to new situations.
- Use "I" phrases to express emotions and thoughts.
- Help others when there is a perceived need.

- Recognize how differences exist in different settings.
- Understand purpose of rules and government.
- Reveal preferences by holding family votes.
- Identify authoritative figures and leaders (e.g., police officers, governors, and mayors).
- Associate with different groups (e.g., families, church communities, and neighborhood friends).
- Identify the name and value of coins.
- Identify different types of jobs and discuss the importance of each one.
- Explain the process of working for money to buy necessary items.
- Experience the process of buying items at a store.
- Explain the purpose of banks.
- Distinguish between a want and a need.
- Identify the rewards of work.
- Use and follow directional words (e.g., up, down, forward, backward, right, and left).
- State home address.
- Interpret basic maps and elements on them.
- Explain how people get from one place to another (e.g., walking, bikes, trains, cars, and planes).
- Identify types of environments (e.g., rural areas have lots of open land, and cities have many buildings).
- Examine the influence of geography on weather.

What's your story?

Preschoolers will start to become acquainted with social studies while learning their own story. So help them to understand their identity by discussing gender, ethnicity, and other cultural characteristics. Let your children know they are part of a family and a community with traditions related to your belief systems, practices, and recreational habits.

Growth in the subject area then continues when kids observe and interact with a wide range of peers and adults in society. As you experience everyday life, study the people, places, and environments. Engage in intentional conversation as related topics come up.

Use children's literature to expose your little one to diverse people groups and to others who have lived in a different time period or setting. Discuss the experiences of people in the story, and examine how they are similar or different from your child's. If you have an opportunity to travel, use it as a way to teach social studies. In which scenario do you think children will learn more—reading about a historical event in a children's book or actually visiting the historical site or museum? Of course, they learn so much more when they actually experience it.

We once visited an iron ore mining operation from the 1800s and our daughter was able to visualize and better comprehend the conditions in which the people lived. She saw firsthand the clothing and the types of tools utilized during the nineteenth century. She was so curious about many of the exhibits and we were able to teach her a lot about history, geography, and diversity. You don't even have to find a museum. You could probably walk down the main street of your town and find historical relics, geographical landmarks, or cultural events.

6

Physical Education: Developing Motor & Movement Skills

No one would argue the importance of developing kids' cognitive abilities before kindergarten. But sometimes we don't maintain the same focus on physical development beyond crawling and walking. In fact, there are many benefits when toddlers and preschoolers exercise muscles and expend significant amounts of energy. They improve overall health, aerobic fitness, cognitive functioning, bone health, self-esteem, and they develop essential motor skills that will help with future school tasks such as cutting paper with scissors.[1]

Interestingly, there is even a relationship between motor skill development with young children and achievement in mathematics and reading. In other words, physical activity connects with brain development. As a result, kids tend to do better in elementary school if they are active during their preschool years.[2]

If you are wondering how much time our little ones should exercise or engage in some sort of physical activity, the Society of Health and Physical Educators (SHAPE) offers some guidelines.[3] Parents and caregivers should engage with and encourage their infants (0 – 12 months) to explore movement for short periods many times each day. You can do this with play mats where babies bat or kick hanging toys, or simply by giving them opportunities to wiggle their arms and legs. Many infants also enjoy grabbing onto linking rings or playing with soft books and teething toys.

For toddlers (12 – 36 months), include daily opportunities to engage in at least 30 minutes of structured physical activity (meaning it's planned and directed), and at least 60 minutes of unstructured or self-directed play. Whether structured or not, all activities should provide an occasion for motor skill and large muscle development. In addition, when toddlers aren't sleeping, they shouldn't be sedentary for more than 60 minutes at a time.

With preschoolers (age 3 – 5 years), the recommended time for physical activity increases to 60 minutes of structured time and at least 60 minutes of unstructured activity. As with any other age group, preschoolers should avoid prolonged periods of sedentary behavior. Simply put, allow your children to participate in some sort of activity on a daily basis. Odds are this is already happening. Your kids are digging in a sand box, playing in the snow, running around outside at the playground, or dancing when you play music. The key is to ensure that they have opportunities to be active for sufficient periods of time. Strive to identify fun activities and create a culture where exercise is valued.

Parental and family practices will influence the degree to which children are physically active.[4] Therefore, be intentional about providing instruction to help your little ones develop knowledge, a positive attitude, and the confidence needed to grow muscles and fine motor skills.

Unfortunately, in the 21st century, children aren't active enough and we have seen reduced amounts of unstructured, free play with kids. In the midst of the "busyness" of life, make it a point to commit time in which your child is able to engage in movement and outdoor play. And provide options when choosing the activity—kids often invent very fun and creative games, rules, and actions.

When thinking about what it means to develop physically, there are three facets to consider.

1. Strengthening the large muscles in arms, shoulders, neck, legs, and mid-section.
2. Increasing fundamental movement skills and muscle control (which includes agility, balance, flexibility, and coordination).
3. Improving fine motor skills to enhance hand-eye co-ordination, dexterity, and the ability to perform every-day activities such as writing and buttoning clothes.

But don't forget, just as kids develop at different rates cognitively, they also display differences as they advance physically. Be sure to include activities and skills that are de-velopmentally appropriate, and introduce them in an easy-to-difficult progression.

Strengthening muscle and locomotive skills

It takes four to six months before infants have control over their muscles, at which point they grow large muscles by grab-bing toys, raising their head, and pushing off the floor. They progress to crawling and then start to develop leg muscle con-trol when closer to a year old. As kids transition into toddler-hood at around age 1, they begin to walk. Soon thereafter, they start to develop the ability to throw, run, hop, and jump. These are all examples of locomotive skills.

Physical development and maturation are parts of the natural growth process, but caregivers also need to help chil-dren learn gross motor skills.[5] Therefore, make observations during play time and look for teachable moments. When our daughter was first learning how to do somersaults as a three-year-old, we showed her how to move her body and explained how to bend at the waist, tuck her chin to her chest, and push with her legs so she wouldn't fall sideways.

Parents can offer assistance when children first learn how to jump (use your arms for balance and bend your knees when landing), throw (lead with your elbow), gallop (keep one leg in front of the other), and catch a ball (squeeze as soon as you feel the ball touch your hands). Your intentionality will facilitate improved locomotive skills. Don't assume toddlers will naturally learn these abilities on their own. Instead, take the time to demonstrate proper technique and physically guide their movements the first few times through. Some children do pick up skills on their own, especially if they imitate you or siblings, but all kids need guidance and the opportunity to practice.

As much as you are able, provide time for outside play. Young children are more likely to develop large muscles and gross motor skills when they have great amounts of space to run, throw, catch, hop, jump, skip, and march. We like to play with rocks near a river or take hikes in the woods. In fact, before our daughter reached her third birthday, she developed the stamina and muscle strength to hike a mile on her own. Of course, we didn't force her, but we did challenge her to go as far as she could without help. If she did tire out, she knew we would be willing to carry her the rest of the way.

If you live in a cold weather climate, preschoolers are far less active during the winter months. As a result, it is important to acquire appropriate gear to enable outside play in the colder temperatures. Caregivers can take kids to the local recreation center or other indoor play areas to provide space to run around when the weather doesn't cooperate.

As your kids increase physical activity they will also develop movement skills. They will improve **coordination** (the ability to use the senses with their body to complete motor tasks accurately), **agility** (the ability to quickly change body position with accuracy), **balance** (maintaining equilibrium while stationary or moving), and **flexibility** (the ability to move their body in a wide range of motion).

To help enhance movement skills in each of the four areas, take a look at the activities on the next two pages. Try to incorporate as many as possible during the daily structured play time. Eventually, kids will start to do many activities on their own during the unstructured times of physical exercise.

Developing balance

- Walk on tip-toes.
- Continuously jump up and down on both feet.
- Continuously jump up and down on one foot.
- Walk on a curb or a narrow object close to the ground.
- Balance on one leg for as long as possible (do this with both the right and left leg).
- Balance on a wide, short box.
- Swing on a swing set.

Developing gross motor skills

- Walk backwards and sideways.
- Pivot in a circle around one foot (try this with both the left and right foot).
- Jump as far as possible from a still position (like a standing long jump).
- Jump as far as possible from a moving position.
- Dance to music and repeat motions to songs such as the "Chicken Dance" or the "Hokey Pokey."
- Hop on both feet and on each foot separately.
- Swim with the aid of a flotation device (you can buy a Puddle Jumper for about $15).
- Play with balls, Frisbees, jump ropes, and Hula Hoops.
- Roll down a hill.
- Climb stairs.
- Ride a tricycle.
- Do somersaults.
- Go on a treasure hunt (geocaching is a fun way to do this).
- Make cards that contain visuals of different activities (e.g., skip, clap, and hop); ask your child to pick a card and then perform the movement for three seconds.
- Play games with movement, such as Hide & Seek; Duck, Duck Goose; Red Light, Green Light; Ring around the Rosie; London Bridge is Falling Down; Simon Says; Follow the Leader; and Mother May I?

- Slide down a slide and interact with others on playground equipment.
- Pull and push wagons, toy vacuums, and objects on a string.

Developing coordination

- Climb a ladder or a mini rock wall on a playground.
- Throw and kick a ball to each other.
- Throw objects into a bucket (the bean bag game is an especially fun activity).
- Walk with a bean bag or small pillow on their head.
- Play with a bouncy ball.
- Roll balls to knock plastic cups or blocks over (create your own bowling game).

Developing flexibility and agility

- Create a fun obstacle course where your child must crawl through a box, go underneath an object, and crawl over objects.
- Practice running, stopping, and then starting again.
- Play on a playground.
- Participate in kids yoga (Cosmic Kids Yoga is a fun option and it is available for free on YouTube).

The key is to take advantage of various opportunities during your daily routines. Ask your child to hop to the dinner table, push a basket of toys back to the play room while cleaning up, or balance on one foot while washing hands.

Improving fine motor skills

During the toddler years, children begin to develop fine motor skills and learn to manipulate toys and objects. Movements with small muscles become more refined, hand-eye coordination improves, and kids become more skilled at performing tasks with their hands. They develop the ability to control utensils such as scissors, pencils, and silverware. At this time, you can introduce games and activities. Spin a spinner, roll dice, make cookies with cookie cutters, and blow bubbles.

When you buy the first bottle of bubbles, your toddlers won't know how to hold the wand and will likely make a mess when trying to reload it with bubble juice. Given instruction, time, and practice, they will soon learn to blow some pretty big bubbles without spilling the entire bottle. Whether blowing bubbles or working on other fine motor skills, parents must model proper technique and actually guide children's fingers, hands, arms, legs, and feet. Demonstrate how to hold crayons, paintbrushes, silverware, and cups until your little one is proficient.

If you reexamine the teaching ideas we included in the previous chapters, you will notice we frequently incorporated manipulatives and other forms of learning involving movement. These kinds of activities were intentionally included because they enhance fine motor skills. For example, you can use tangram pieces to help teach geometry, and you can encourage play with mini-puzzles to learn science concepts. Not only do the activities help children learn specific subject-area content, but they also improve hand-eye coordination and dexterity.

Other kinesthetic learning activities could include reading books and singing songs that incorporate movement. Our daughter's favorite song at one point was "Itsy-Bitsy Spider." When she first sang it with the corresponding movements as a two-year-old, she had a difficult time connecting her thumbs to her pointer-fingers and then alternating them as the spider "went up the water spout." After about a month of singing and practicing the movements, she soon had the ability to do it successfully. Below are some other things you can ask your preschooler to do to improve fine motor skills.

Developing fine motor skills

- Trace letters, numbers, and pictures.

- Connect the dots.
- "Follow the path" where you must draw within a pair of curved lines (draw two curvy lines that parallel each other, and then ask your child to draw a third curvy line in between).
- Draw basic pictures of a face.
- Manipulate Play-Doh, clay, and bread dough by pounding, rolling, making cookie cutouts, and squeezing.
- Work on buttons, zippers, Velcro attachments, and snaps.
- Cut with child-sized, safety scissors (with supervision).
- Use tweezers or tongs to pick up objects (there is a fun game called The Sneaky Snacky Squirrel where kids must pick up acorns with a "squirrel squeezer").
- Open clothespins and place them where desired.
- Thread beads, noodles, buttons, or cereal onto string.
- Practice tying a basic knot.
- Act out plays and songs with finger puppets.
- Put together age-appropriate jigsaw puzzles.
- Play with Lego Duplos (or other similar toys where they have to connect and pull apart pieces).
- Use funnels and other containers to practice pouring and filling water or sand.
- Hit a balloon into the air repeatedly.
- Take stickers off the page and place them in a desired location.
- Practice gripping, drawing, and coloring with crayons, chalk, and colored pencils.
- Close zip-lock baggies.
- Dress dolls and play pretend kitchen.
- Use water-color paints to paint strokes, shapes, and figures.
- Sprinkle glitter and use glue sticks and tape with crafts.
- Play with building blocks.

While playing, make sure the materials you're letting young children use are age-appropriate and safe. And that you are closely supervising. Certainly, you wouldn't want to give two-year-olds small blocks if they still tend to put things in their mouth. You wouldn't want them to play with balloons or baggies unsupervised because of the choking hazard, and you'll want to make sure your walls don't get marked up with crayons.

As a final note, parents can help build fine motor skills while kids learn to clean up. They make glorious messes, and you can use the opportunity to teach skills such as washing materials, taking care of toys, and putting them in the proper place.

Physical education standards for preschool children

Parents often wonder when young children are developmentally able to reach various fine and gross motor milestones. Before we offer standards, we want to again stress that each child is unique. As with math, science, literacy, and social studies, everyone will grow physically at different rates. However, the list below includes when children are likely to develop each skill.

Birth – 12 months

- Move arms and legs.
- Reach for and bat at hanging items with hands and feet.
- Wiggle and squirm on the floor.
- Grab objects.
- Squeeze your finger (when you place your finger against baby's hand).
- Pinch objects with thumb and index finger.
- Transfer objects from hand to hand.
- Develop the ability to sit up (generally between 4 and 8 months).
- Play pat-a-cake.
- Roll over (generally between 4 and 8 months).

- Crawl (generally between 6 and 10 months).
- Pull to stand up (generally between 6 and 10 months).

12 – 24 months

- Begin walking (generally between 10 and 16 months).
- Hold a book and turn pages properly.
- Stretch out (such as touching toes and bending sideways).
- Squeeze, grasp, and pinch.
- Shovel in the sand.
- Climb stairs using one foot at a time, and hands.
- Kick a ball.

2 – 3 years old

- Recognize vocabulary related with movement (e.g., run, hop, skip, walk, and throw).
- Catch a large ball and throw with aim.
- Develop the ability to kick a ball in a desired direction.
- Walk on tip-toes.
- Put on and remove clothes.
- Balance on one foot for at least five seconds.
- Walk backwards and sideways.
- Dance to music.
- Climb stairs using alternate feet.
- Jump up and squat down.
- Jump over small objects with both feet.
- Develop the ability to go over, under, and in-between objects.
- Develop hand and finger dexterity (e.g., use tweezers, clothespins, and scissors).
- Ride a tricycle.
- Write, trace, and color between the lines.
- Paint and draw elementary pictures.
- Increase development and skill with gross motor activities such as running, hopping, marching, and dancing.
- Climb on a short ladder on playground equipment.

4 – 6 years old

- Balance on one leg for longer periods of time.
- Ride a bike.
- Throw and catch with accuracy.
- Fall and tumble in such a way as to prevent injury (e.g., gymnastics).
- Practice skipping (which requires balance, rhythm, and coordination).
- Learn how to swim.
- Increase awareness of their placement in relation to the people and things around them.
- Increase balance on large motor equipment.
- Catch a ball with increased consistency.
- Use household tools (e.g., scissors, glue, and tape) independently to complete a task.
- Improve hand-eye coordination.
- Increase the ability to use fingers and hands to manipulate items.
- Walk on tip-toes for longer distances.

Reaching the goals

So what can you do to help your toddler and preschooler meet these physical education standards? Here are four practical suggestions.

1. **Start by setting a good example.** If parents and caregivers are active, then children will see the value of physical vitality.
2. **Proactively teach proper movements to develop confidence.** Children may not be inclined to nurture their own development in some areas, so you might have to provide detailed instruction and encouragement.
3. **Avoid too much television.** Childhood obesity rates are going up partly because of increased screen time

and the subsequent lack of physical activity. (Rates are also increasing because of unhealthy eating habits.) Even when children are active, it is often for very short periods of time and without the necessary rigor.[6]

4. **Provide safe areas in which to play outside.** They will have more room to run and exercise. If you feel it isn't safe for your little ones to be outdoors alone, then go outside with them.

Just as young kids are inherently curious, they also have a lot of energy. Take advantage of their desire to play and provide ample time for activity. Not only will children grow muscle and improve motor skills, but you will also improve the child-parent relationship. Each time you engage in activity together you increase communication and develop a stronger bond. It is such a joy to watch kids play and help them to feel special through shared activity. Don't miss out by limiting these types of opportunities.

7

Creative Expression: Fostering Artistic Talent & Appreciation

Former president of the National Art Education Association and retired Stanford professor, Elliot Eisner, understood the importance of developing imaginative young minds and artistic abilities. He envisioned an educational system that had an increased focus on creative expression, and his quote summarizes what caregivers should emphasize when teaching children.

"I am talking about a culture in which more importance is placed on exploration than on discovery, more value is assigned to surprise than to control, more attention is devoted to what is distinctive than to what is standard, more interest is related to what is metaphorical than to what is literal. It is an educational culture that has a greater focus on becoming than on being, and places more value on the imaginative than on the factual."[1]

Just as parents and teachers often minimize the value of physical development, many do not highlight the artistic aspects of education that Eisner describes. This is unfortunate, because when toddlers and preschoolers have opportunities to think creatively the benefits are many. First, engaging in art projects and activities will nurture children's social-emotional skills. They improve their self-confidence and learn to be more self-expressive. And because art projects often involve others, children will increase their ability to share and take turns.

Second, there is a correlation between art education and cognitive growth. More specifically, the arts bolster language development and academic skills in math and science. Perhaps this isn't surprising, since math and science educators often place such a high value on the process and not just the end result.

Third, both the visual and performing arts enhance motor skills. While painting, coloring, playing an instrument, or crafting, your children improve visual-spatial skills, hand-eye coordination, and fine muscle control. Furthermore, while dancing to music or acting out a scene from a book, they develop gross motor skills.

Fourth, when you give kids opportunities to explore the arts you foster an appreciation for the beauty around us. There are so many amazing works of art—both in human-made creations and the natural world. Exposure to this beauty produces a profound sense of joy and gratitude.

Fifth, the creative part of the brain often makes connections to the linguistic and logical areas of the brain. Exposing your child to the visual and performing arts will then support other disciplines, including language arts and social studies. Finally, and perhaps most obviously, art will enhance your children's creative abilities.[2]

What does a preschool education in the arts include? The next two sections talk about important lessons in the visual and performing arts.

Visual arts

There is a difference between completing a craft and doing a true visual art project. Crafts tend to have a predetermined end result. While there are benefits when you do crafts with your little ones, it is also important to allow for their own freedom of expression. Let them create whatever they want on occasion and try not to always be concerned about the end product. Instead, give them a chance to use their imaginations and make their own decisions.

The process is important and kids will learn through experimentation. Therefore, ask open-ended questions such as, "How can we make an animal?" "What materials would you like to use?" "What colors would you like to include?" "What if we used this design?" "Do you want to create a pattern?" When children are able to make these types of choices, they will be more likely to reap the benefits we discussed in the previous section.

The visual arts include drawing, painting, coloring, printing, sculpting Play-Doh, creating a collage, using textiles, modeling, printmaking, stringing beads, and just about any other construction. When your children engage in these activities, teach related vocabulary and talk about the basic elements and principles of art, including:[3]

- **Shapes**: Connect artwork with math terms. Talk about symmetry or include geometric shapes such as rectangular, circular, linear, or curvy designs. It is helpful to use an anchor chart that kids can use as a reference. (An anchor chart is a graphic representation displaying the various shapes.)
- **Texture**: Some creations will be soft and fuzzy, while others will be coarse or smooth. Connect your child's creations with the senses and include many different words to describe texture.
- **Color**: The primary colors include red, yellow, and blue. Secondary colors are an equal mixture of two primary colors, resulting in green, purple, and orange. When you use a lot of complementary colors (such as red with green), you can create a vibrant look. Contrast light colors with dark, bright with soft, and point out the warm colors of a beautiful sunset or other images.

- **Space**: Create and examine both two- and three-dimensional shapes. Discuss elements such as foreground and background, perspective, and illusion.
- **Emotion:** When looking at pieces of art, what thoughts come to mind? Is it calming? Is it vibrant and cheery? Do the lines on a face indicate anger, sadness, or happiness?
- **Structure:** Does the art work rely on repetition? Is it balanced? Is it proportional or symmetrical? What types of patterns are visible?

You can discuss these principles and encourage development in the visual arts by reading books together that include various shapes, textures, and colors. In addition, expose preschoolers to different art forms by visiting an art exhibit at a local college (many are free), a museum, or an art gallery. While at the exhibit, ask your child's opinion about a sculpture, painting, or photograph. What colors does he like? What shapes does he see? What emotions come to mind? How is one piece similar to or different than another?

In fact, you don't even have to leave your house to do this. Simply find artistic creations on the Internet. As you view art work, discuss what you see and talk about the possible meanings of each image.

Another way to help your kids to think about the processes of art is to provide time for them to express their own creativity. Let them experiment with a variety of tools and resources, such as paintbrushes, chalk, clay, construction paper, pictures, crayons, easels, cutting utensils, and a camera. (Again, be sure to make age-appropriate decisions.) Use food coloring or watercolor paint to mix colors. Take pictures with your phone and then analyze the images. Create works of art reflecting an experience, or something seen or heard. For instance, toddlers love to create a paper cutout of animals after visiting a zoo or watching a show about animals.

Lastly, make connections between art and other subjects. You can easily connect art with math by talking about geometric shapes or counting objects in a photograph. You will automatically connect it with literacy as you include new art-related vocabulary words. There is a lot of beauty in science, and you can point out the symmetry, shape, array of color, and texture of a flower while introducing its biological structure.

Performing arts

Some aspects of the performing arts include dance, theater, and music. At birth, start with music. As caregivers sing lullabies and sway to the rhythm of a tune, infants will begin to recognize tone, rhythmic patterns, and tempo.[4] As an added benefit, parents who sing while cuddling with little ones will promote attachment.[5] At preschool age, early music education will connect with increased cognitive functioning and overall academic achievement.[6]

When children listen to or engage in musical activities, advanced imaging technologies indicate that their brains "light up like a Christmas tree in many different areas."[7] Movement and rhythmic exercises will also stimulate their brains. Exposure is sometimes thought to be the most beneficial between the ages of two and six, so these artistic endeavors are especially advantageous to incorporate before kindergarten.[8]

Accentuate the performing arts by singing, humming, playing instruments, and by simply listening to songs. Listen to a broad variety of music, including classical pieces, children's contemporary pop, and music from different cultures and time periods. (When applicable, be sure to prescreen lyrics to ensure that they are age-appropriate.) It is also amusing to make up songs. We would create "clean up" songs to help encourage our daughter to pick up the mess in her room, and she would make up words to the tune of "Twinkle, Twinkle Little Star" and "The Wheels on the Bus."

Here are a dozen other enjoyable ways parents can include the performing arts in everyday activities.

1. **Use bells, musical toys, and homemade instruments to create music.** Babies love shaking a closed container filled with rice, or banging on a tambourine.

2. **Play music that includes movement.** Songs like the "Chicken Dance" not only help with motor skills, but also teach children about tempo. Furthermore, clapping or stomping to the beat of music helps develop rhythm. Sing songs quietly and loudly, quickly or slowly. Move or dance accordingly.

3. **Ask your child to reenact different roles and everyday experiences.** Pretend to be a doctor with a patient, a mom with a baby, a parent driving a car, or someone emailing on a computer. Include props to enhance the experience.

4. **Show pictures of different musical instruments and describe the varying sounds they make.** Even better, acquire a few instruments to have around the house. Watch for garage sales, where you might see an inexpensive guitar or drum set.

5. **When your toddler plays with dolls or stuffed animals, create a story.** For example, young kids often act out the events of a picnic when playing with toys.

6. **Create a little theater area in your living room by including props and costumes.** Once the stage is set, ask your child to act out a scene from a book or a show.

7. **Create or buy puppets and act out a scene.** Finger puppets and plays are especially fun.

8. **When reading books, take time to ask questions about the characters.** Discuss the roles and emotions of the people in the story.

9. **Make up dance moves.** Your toddler will love to dance with dolls and stuffed animals.

10. **Video record your child dancing, singing, or acting.** Then watch and talk about their artistic creations. These videos will be wonderful ways to preserve memories, too.

11. **Imitate different noises and sounds.** See if your young learners can mimic animals and other noises they hear in nature.
12. **Use the arts as a way to express love.** Create fun birthday cards for the grandparents, sing songs to show affection, and make creative gifts for friends.

As you engage in the performing arts, give your children the freedom to choose the music, dance movements, and creative props. Incorporate tunes or stories with different moods, tempos, pitches, volume levels, and rhythms.

You can also help build a strong foundation if you include popular songs such as "Head, Shoulders, Knees and Toes." This song, as well as the ABC song, will foster artistic development and serve as excellent memory aids for other content areas.

To further support your own creative juices, we have included some of our favorite activities related to both the visual and performing arts. We encourage you to find some of your own favorites.

Creative art activities

Decorate cookies   Age: 2 – 6
Subtopic: Visual arts; color and shape
Directions: Buy cookie cutters, bake sugar cookies, and decorate with frosting. Use a variety of colors and designs with the frosting.

Texture collage   Age: 3 – 6
Subtopic: Visual arts; creative expression; texture
Directions: Collect a variety of materials from around the house or from the craft store (such as pipe cleaners, pompoms, popsicle sticks, wiggly eyes, empty paper towel and toilet paper tubes, empty oatmeal containers, tissue paper, glitter, colored paper, glue, tape, and scissors). Choose a few items

and let your child loose to see what she dreams up. This is an open-ended activity allowing for creativity and self-expression. With younger children, supervision and discussion play a key part. When children are old enough to use scissors and glue unsupervised, then they can be free to create independently.

Create a pan flute   Age: 3 – 5

Subtopic: Music and crafts
Directions: You will need large straws, scissors, a ruler, and tape. Cut the first straw to be 20 centimeters long. Make each subsequent straw two centimeters shorter and then tape eight together. Blow across the straws and you should hear different pitches.

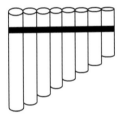

Magazine faces   Age: 3 – 4

Subtopic: Visual arts
Directions: You will need magazines, scissors, paper, and glue. Cut out or have your child cut out various eyes, noses, mouths, eye brows, mustaches, and ears from magazines. Create funny faces by gluing them on paper.

Paint with household items   Age: 3 – 5

Subtopic: Visual arts; color and texture; creative expression
Directions: You will need tempura paint, construction paper, and various items for painting. Focus on shape and texture, such as empty toilet paper tubes folded into different shapes; potatoes and other vegetables cut in half for stamping; cotton balls, tin foil, feathers, pipe cleaners, Q-tips, bubble wrap,

sponges, or anything else you have around the house to make unique textures. Choose three or four "paint brushes" and start with the primary colors, which include red, yellow, and blue. Talk about and mix colors to make new colors. Discuss the different items you chose for painting, and discuss shape and texture. Let your child have free rein to create while asking questions about what she is doing.

Create a puzzle   Age: 2 – 4

Subtopic: Visual arts; photography
Directions: Take some fun photos with your phone or digital camera. Pick your favorite three or four and print out a copy of each one. Cut them into the desired number of pieces using unique cuts as seen below. The younger the child, the fewer pieces you should cut.

The Internet has many other ideas you could incorporate with your toddler or preschooler. As you identify activities, keep in mind the developmental stages and standards.

Creative expression standards for preschool children

Birth – 12 months

During this age, parents should:
- Sing lullabies to children.

- Play music and observe baby's reactions.
- Rock and sway to the beat of a tune.
- Move baby's arms and legs to the tempo and the beat of music.
- Tell stories with music.

12 – 24 months

Your children should begin to learn how to:
- Paint and draw abstract pictures.
- Pound on play pianos and drums.
- Identify colors.
- Make different noises and sounds with their voices.
- Listen to musical performances (both instrumental and vocal).
- Pretend play.
- Recognize rhyming words.

2 – 3 years old

Your children should begin to learn how to:
- Properly handle art tools (e.g., paint brushes, pencils, and crayons).
- Dance to music.
- Participate during singing activities (e.g., perform body movements or move a stuffed animal to music).
- Sing songs and repeat lyrics.
- Identify different textures (e.g., smooth, bumpy, rough, prickly, and fuzzy).
- Create representations of objects with materials (e.g., use Play-Doh to make a cookie, or blocks to create a garage).
- Identify similarities and differences between artistic creations.
- Build basic structures with blocks, boxes, Legos, or other items.
- Act out movements of animals.
- Use songs to tell a story.

- Recognize tunes from songs (e.g., recognize the ABC tune if someone hums it).
- Identify songs that are fast versus slow, loud versus soft, funny versus serious.
- Move to the rhythm, tempo, and beat of a song.
- Create and play their own instruments (e.g., use a Tupperware container as a drum).
- Role play everyday experiences (e.g., taking a doll's temperature, buying items at a grocery store, and feeding a baby a bottle).
- Creatively move their body by dancing, hopping, swaying, clapping, twisting, or turning.
- Respond to events of plays and movies.
- Imitate roles from the child's everyday experiences.
- Identify color, shape, and texture.

4 – 6 years old

Your children should begin to learn how to:
- Act out a scene with finger puppets.
- Make up their own words to songs.
- Create rhyming words.
- Identify different types of instruments.
- Experiment with traditional and non-traditional musical instruments (e.g., bells, metal cans, and pan flutes).
- Recognize different types of music and tunes from different cultures.
- Act out a story or experience.
- Recognize that mixing colors produces another color.
- Express opinions about artistic creations, such as paintings and music.
- Copy basic pictures.
- Compare and contrast different types of sounds and music.
- Express stories and ideas in numerous ways (e.g., drawings, dramatic representations, and modeling).
- Create rhythmic patterns with voice, body movements, or an instrument.

- Develop musical preferences and articulate why they like certain types.
- Represent real-life and imaginary events through dramatic play, using props and costumes.
- Assume the role of a fictitious character in a book, movie, or play, and speak in a voice and manner that represents the character.
- Express feelings, words, and ideas with creative movement.
- Imitate dance moves and learn basic dance steps.
- Compare and contrast different forms of dance.
- Recognize different types of art forms, such as photographs, paintings, drawings, and sculptures.

Connect art with daily life

We were once at a park with our three-year-old daughter, and she found a series of large playground drums, chimes, and bells. She literally played them for over twenty minutes while Mom, Dad, Grandma, and Grandpa watched. To be honest, all the adults got pretty bored after about five minutes. But our daughter loved beating the variously sized drums, and investigating how size influenced the pitch and sound.

It is essential to provide opportunities for your little ones to participate in the arts, similar to our experience at the playground. As early as infancy, cultivate artistic expression and creativity by engaging in the performing and visual arts on a regular basis.

If you were to observe a day-care center, preschool class, or kid's church program, you will almost always see children singing or participating in some sort of art project. That is because art engages kids, and the leaders properly value creative expression as much as the other subject areas.

Art often enhances knowledge and abilities in math, reading, science, and social studies, so it is important for caregivers to integrate the arts as they teach other academic skills.

Create fun representations of numbers, draw pictures of scientific ideas, turn a piece of literature into a play, and look at pictures of people from different cultures. This type of teaching makes everything more meaningful, fun, and memorable.

8

Character Is Higher Than Intellect

The title of this chapter is a quote from Ralph Waldo Emerson, and many would agree that character education is a crucial element of school preparedness. In education and the workplace today there is an increased focus on developing skills to help people effectively function in their environment and interact well with others. These skills are known as "soft skills" and they include one's personal attributes, behaviors, character traits, and attitudes.

Yes, teaching students math, science, and reading content is imperative. But teaching them to follow directions, sit quietly, and be patient is also essential. When parents raise kind, selfless, gritty, and obedient kids they will successfully and positively contribute to their classroom community. Elementary school educators agree that children are more likely to succeed in school when parents are intentional about developing these types of behaviors.[1]

Just as we teach kids to count to ten, balance on one foot, identify the sounds of letters, and draw a straight line, we can mold and shape character early in life. Developing a work ethic, the ability to persevere, and other similar soft skills will help in all arenas of life. Children will be able to more effectively interact with people at a family picnic, at church, on a team, and later as an employee.

It's all about the environment you create

It's important to think about the environments we create in our homes, and the type of mindset we instill in our little ones. Parents, relatives, and others in your social circles can aid or hinder your child's character development just as they do with cognitive growth. If there is a culture of kindness in your home, then children will likely grow up to be kind people. If you strive to have a positive attitude and outlook on life, then your preschooler will probably adopt the same mindset. If you speak with grace in frustrating circumstances, then your child will do the same. Conversely, if parents are impatient, self-centered, or rude, then there is an increased chance that their children will take on the same behaviors.

As school teachers who were involved with hundreds of parent-teacher conferences, we saw examples of this often. For instance, I (Jeff) once had a student named Kenzie who was pleasant, caring, and kind. Then I met Kenzie's parents at a conference and understood why she had such a positive demeanor. Her parents had the same friendly disposition. On the other hand, another student by the name of Micah was often negative and snippy in class. Unfortunately, Micah's parents were also somewhat unpleasant during our meeting. We could fill an entire chapter with similar stories pointing to the importance of the type of culture caregivers cultivate in their homes.

We all must be intentional about the environment we create. Annie and I are very mindful of our own actions because, if we don't think about it, we know we would have the tendency to pass on negative behaviors and attitudes. If we're ready to yell at our toddler because of her inappropriate behavior, we take a minute to calm down and collect our thoughts so we can firmly address the misbehavior with grace and kindness. If we're ungrateful about something, then we try to redirect our attitude by thinking about something for which we are thankful. If we become impatient because something isn't working the way we expected it to, we try to step aside and think about how we can solve the problem so she might learn to be persistent as well.

While we strive to cultivate positive characteristics and attitudes, we often fall short. We know we aren't going to be perfect, but we simply do our best. And when we do fail, we have intentional conversations with our child regarding how we could have had a better response or attitude.

If you are concerned that another person might be a bad influence on your kids you can counteract that influence with your own actions, and by talking about proper conduct and attitudes soon after a negative experience. We definitely don't want to develop an elitist mindset or start to think we are too good for others, but we are quick to correct our daughter when she adopts poor behaviors.

We want to create an atmosphere in which she learns about and adopts a wide array of positive character traits, and the culture we primarily attempt to establish in our home aligns with our values and belief systems. Therefore, we try to stress virtues such as love, joy, peace, patience, kindness, goodness, gentleness, and self-control.[2] Each family is unique, so think about the values you might want to pass on and then be deliberate about how you live and what you say.

Attributes and traits that lead to success in the classroom

Teachers also create a set of goals involving the soft skills. There are specific behaviors and attitudes they hope to cultivate—which in turn will produce an effective learning environment.

Develop a strong work ethic

My (Jeff) family would visit my grandfather on a fairly regular basis growing up, and I can still remember how hard he worked. He would wake up early every day, blast American march music (to wake me up so I would help), and start working on house projects or other tasks. Through his actions he helped to instill a solid work ethic in me.

Teachers often express concern because students aren't completing homework or sticking with an activity for longer than a handful of minutes. As parents, we have the amazing power to instill a work ethic that teachers and future employers would appreciate. We simply need to model hard work and talk about its benefits. And there are many advantages, including a sense of dignity, a sense of accomplishment, the possibility of blessing others through our work, and the reward of seeing results.

We're not expecting our two- or three-year-old to clean up a huge mess entirely, but we will require her to help and be responsible. You can begin as early as infancy to teach your children about responsibility. When your infant can sit up and grasp a toy, she can begin to put toys back in the basket at the end of play time. Model the desired action while saying, "It's time to clean up the toys," and then be quick to offer help when needed.

As a four-year-old, our child still required support from time to time, but for the most part she knew where everything should go and was able to clean up independently. Additionally, she loved to help with house cleaning tasks. We made it a natural part of our day to dust, sweep, do the dishes, and assist in other ways that fit her ability. She completed many age-appropriate tasks around the house and continued to bear more responsibility and contribute to the functions of our household as she grew.

Dave Ramsey, financial and workplace expert, summarized it best by stating, "You should view teaching your children to work in the same way you view teaching them to bathe and brush their teeth—as a necessary skill for life."[3] So think of developmentally appropriate chores and consider establishing a solid work ethic in your children early. Work shouldn't be seen as a negative thing; instead, try to make it fun by singing or turning tasks into games.

Encourage curiosity and critical thinking

One of my (Annie) favorite mental pictures of our little girl is her tiny body crouched down, looking intently at something she had discovered on the ground. Her chubby little fingers were exploring her world and seeking to gather new information as a two-year-old. A child's desire to learn is innate, and all we have to do as parents is foster this sense of curiosity.

The endless questions of a child can be exhausting, but the need to make sense of the world is what drives those inquiries. However, when we answer questions with questions of our own we help to get children to work through some of their own answers. We develop critical thinkers and problem solvers. By guiding kids through a difficult task with suggestions and strategies—instead of doing it for them—we are teaching them to become confident in their own abilities.

Promote empathy, kindness, and selflessness

These traits can be hard for anyone, but particularly for toddlers and preschoolers who think they are the center of the universe. If you consider developmental capabilities, kids under three won't realistically understand empathy, but there are many things you can do to help a child begin to see how others are feeling in certain situations. You can read books about emotions while making observations about facial expressions seen in the pictures. You could call your child's attention to the feelings of others to help open her mind to different emotions.

After a play date, we often ask our daughter how she was a kind and loving friend instead of asking if she had fun. We want her to have fun, but we also want to emphasize selfless interactions with friends.

Another way to promote kindness and selflessness is to encourage children to share with siblings and friends. Again, sharing is not necessarily a concept toddlers will completely grasp, because they are still developing the ability to see life outside of themselves. But as you demonstrate empathy, model sharing, and have discussions with your children, they will begin to make connections.

You might be familiar with *Daniel Tiger's Neighborhood,* an excellent kid's show based on the popular PBS broadcast, *Mr. Roger's Neighborhood.* There is an episode in which Daniel does not want to share his new stickers with his sister, but he soon learns that playing together can be fun for everyone.

Frequently, children see sharing as a difficult thing to do, so talk with your child about the benefits of cooperation. When kids share they can make friends, they can make someone else happy, it will teach them kindness, and as seen in the show it is often more enjoyable to play together.

If you are like us you have probably heard your little one say something such as "I want a cracker" in a demanding tone. All children do it, and we believe it's important to teach our daughter to ask for things in a way that is kind. It's not as simple as just reminding her to say please. We need to explain to her why a rude tone is unacceptable and then give her words so she can express herself in a better way.

When she is disrespectful or demanding, we comment on her disposition and quietly remind her to "Please say it in a different way." We try not to cater to a selfish child. Instead we strive to teach her to be considerate and patient while she waits for her request to be answered.

Train them to be patient

We are all familiar with a child's need to have something immediately. When we are talking with other adults and our daughter comes running to tell us something, we attempt to train her to be respectful of our conversation and patiently wait her turn. We set up nonverbal communication cues so she is able to let us know she needs something. We then indicate that we see her, but we need her to wait for the appropriate time. She must understand her desires aren't always going to take center stage.

At the same time, we acknowledge that her needs are valid and we will address them in time. In a similar scenario, if she is playing with other kids and wants a toy another child is playing with, we would ask her to wait her turn.

In kindergarten, teachers sometimes have up to thirty students (or more) in class, and it's simply impossible to immediately attend to the demands of each child in all circumstances. When kindergarteners patiently wait until the teacher is able to help, the whole class will function at an increased level.

Closely connected with developing patience in children is teaching them to exhibit self-control. Effective students will sit still in class, quietly listen to their teacher, think about the consequences of their actions, and patiently work through difficult situations. When parents foster this kind of self-control, children will achieve at higher rates in school and will improve experiences in many other social settings.[4]

Teach them why we need to follow directions

We all want our children to listen and obey. In school, students must understand that teachers create classroom rules to help things run more smoothly. In life, it's important for them to know that there are authority figures who generally strive to take care of and do what's best for everyone.

Part of teaching obedience is setting clear boundaries with understandable expectations, and then following through with consequences after a bad decision. And when children do make a poor decision, they have the ability to be brought back into a right relationship. A child shouldn't be labeled as a bad person based on a single action, but as someone who made a wrong choice.

Instill a thankful heart

A cherished memory for me (Annie) is sitting around a large dinner table at family gatherings with Grandma and Grandpa and all my aunts, uncles, and cousins recounting our gratitude. My uncles and older cousins could easily reduce us all to tears of laughter with hilarious stories of the past. But inevitably, there were also sweet stories of thanks that choked us with emotion. My cousins and I all have families of our own now, and have long since outgrown Grandma's dinner table, but I want to cultivate that same sense of thankfulness in our child. And not just during family functions but throughout her life.

Given the frenetic pace at which we tend to live our lives, a precious part of our young family's routine is the time spent before bed, snuggled up on the couch, talking about the day's events and the things for which we are thankful. It seems like such a small thing, and often our three-year-old is thankful for the things she sees around the room (like the TV remote), but that still sows small seeds of gratitude in her heart.

We can also shape a thankful mindset when we teach our children to give back and think about others. While the holidays can often be a catalyst to look for ways to serve, think about how you can help others throughout the year. The list below might give you some ideas, and many can be done with young children. Not only will you serve your community, but you will cultivate an attitude of compassion and kindness.

- Box up gently used clothing to donate to your local family shelter, refugee center, or charity thrift store.
- Donate kids' craft kits to a local children's hospital, or bring gently used board games and cards to a local homeless shelter.
- Visit a local nursing home in your community. Bring games, crafts, or books to spend an afternoon bringing joy to the people living there. Be sure to call the nursing home in advance to make arrangements for how your family can best help.
- Give a gift to your favorite charity. Find a cause that is dear to your heart and aligns with your values.
- Have children color pictures for Color a Smile (colorasmile.org).
- Sponsor a child through a reputable organization.
- Go through the toys your kids don't play with anymore and give to those who might need them more.
- Help out at a local food pantry, or offer to donate non-perishable food items.

When we teach our children to look to the needs of those around them—rather than to their own needs—we raise grateful, not entitled children. Author Randy Alcorn talks about pitfalls related to those who have a sense of entitlement. "We live in a culture where there is a spirit of entitlement—where we think we deserve all of these great things. If something doesn't go our way, we feel like we've been robbed and deprived. And even when a person gets what they think they're already entitled to, they're not grateful for it. After all, 'I deserve it!'"[5]

Additionally, Alcorn noticed how ungrateful people are quick to inappropriately blame, condemn, and judge others. But we can combat entitlement by creating a culture of thankfulness and empathy in our homes. Try to reflect on the things for which you are thankful and be appreciative of what you do have. You will then develop a proper life perspective with your kids.

Raise gritty kids

Albert Einstein once said, "It's not that I'm so smart, it's just that I stay with problems longer." This quote gets at the essence of the definition of grit, which is someone's ability to persist and achieve goals despite any setbacks he or she might face. Gritty kids will follow through and complete tasks even if the activity isn't necessarily pleasurable, or when it doesn't produce an instant reward.

Another way to think about this idea is to consider the following quote from Winston Churchill. "Success is stumbling from failure to failure with no loss of enthusiasm." The ability to stick with tasks despite failure along the way is a character trait that has consistently proven to be valuable in school and in life.[6]

What can we do to develop grit in our children? Start by challenging them. When our daughter was a little over two years old we would routinely ask her to try buttoning up her own shirt. At first, her little fingers weren't quite able to do it, but we would continually encourage her to try. We have also challenged her to work through conflicts with friends (usually related to sharing), put clothes on her dolls, and walk up steeper hills in the woods. We wouldn't challenge her in ways that were too advanced for her age, but we also wouldn't swoop in and do things for her as soon as she started to get frustrated. Instead, we offered strategies to help, encouraged her to keep trying, and then provided assistance only after it appeared as though she wasn't developmentally ready.

A similar way to develop gritty kids is to provide opportunities to work on long-term goals.[7] The first time our three-year-old tried hopping on one foot, she could hop only once. She kept working on it over the course of three months and eventually, she was able to hop five or six times on the one foot. She is proficient at hopping on her right (dominant) foot and we are now challenging her to work on her left (non-dominant) foot. Writing numbers and letters, learning to draw shapes, and coloring within the lines are additional examples of long-term goals toddlers can work to accomplish.

Give your kids a chance to work on challenging tasks that are age-appropriate. If your child stumbles along the way, keep an optimistic mindset, encourage her, provide appropriate guidance, and help her to overcome frustration. Turn any perceived or real failure into a positive situation by using it as an opportunity to learn. Encourage her to see tasks through to completion, and regularly tell her she will continue to grow and get better. Do these things and you will develop gritty children who will be more successful in school.[8]

Encourage respectful behaviors

Probably the most common classroom decree at any grade level is simply to be respectful. This includes using respectful words, being mindful of others' personal property and classroom materials, and following the Golden Rule. If we can teach our children to treat others the way they themselves want to be treated, classrooms are able to function at a high level. Therefore, create guidelines at home so your little one will know what it means to respect the rules of a future kindergarten class.

Some easy to implement rules at home include keeping hands to yourself, helping pick up toys, and avoiding the temptation to interrupt when others are talking. In many cases, it starts with teaching your kids to respect their own toys and the possessions of your home. Teach them to handle objects with care and avoid engaging in destructive actions, such as drawing on walls with crayons.

Of course, kids are going to make bad decisions and ruin household items, but we simply need to give a consequence and then talk about how we can better respect our possessions. In addition, respect often goes hand in hand with obedience. When we tell our daughter to come up the stairs and she calls back in an exasperated tone, she may be obeying with her actions but she's not doing it in a respectful way.

Finally, we can develop respectful children by talking about how all people are valued. This starts with us, the parents. If our daughter needs our attention, we try to set aside whatever we are doing so we can give our full attention to her and actively listen to her concerns. This is easier said than done because electronic devices are a constant distraction. But we want her to know she is valued and is more important than a phone app or work.

Fostering character and the soft skills

What can parents do to develop positive traits, behaviors, or other characteristics deemed important by your family? Below are some practical strategies.

Model them

This idea certainly connects with the environment you create in your home. If you model poor behaviors, then your children will see your example and learn those same behaviors.

Conversely, if your children see you act with good character, then they will follow that example too.

Edgar A. Guest wrote a great poem entitled, "I'd Rather See a Sermon," that poignantly summarizes this idea. One stanza states . . .

> I soon can learn to do it if you'll let me see it done;
> I can watch your hands in action, but your tongue too fast may run.
> And the lecture you deliver may be very wise and true, but I'd rather get my lessons by observing what you do.

The poem ends by stating, "I might misunderstand the advice you give, but there's no misunderstanding how you act and how you live."[9]

If we happen to model poor behaviors and attitudes along the way, we simply must strive to model an appropriate response. When we show our children that we also make mistakes, but then seek forgiveness and apologize, we teach them so much. It shows that we don't expect perfection or complete mastery. Instead, we all seek to make better choices.

Since our children will never be perfect, we also want to stress that their behavior shouldn't necessarily be seen as a reflection of us. We certainly influence our kids, but we will never eradicate all of the misbehaviors. The goal is to teach lessons so a child's heart will desire the right things for the right reasons.

Talk about your values

Don't underestimate the value of regular communication, especially in this electronic age. Researchers who have studied device usage and caregiver relationships note how parents tend to be less responsive and have fewer conversations with their children because of the tendency to get absorbed with a smart phone.[10] Kids need our attention and will grow if caregivers talk about what it means to display positive characteristics on a regular basis.

Have conversations about the benefits of being kind, caring, curious, selfless, patient, gritty, and respectful. Talk about people in your social circles who possess the same qualities and characteristics you value. Discuss different scenarios your kids see on television or in movies. As previously mentioned, the PBS Kid's show, *Daniel Tiger's Neighborhood*, is an excellent cartoon that can facilitate many good discussions. Also read children's books that focus on soft skills and character development. Below includes a small sampling of ideas.

- *Giraffes Can't Dance* (grit & perseverance)
- *The Way I Act* (developing character)
- *Bear Says Thanks* (gratitude & kindness)
- *It's Mine!* (sharing & generosity)
- *The Little Red Hen* (hard work)
- *An Awesome Book of Thanks!* (gratitude)
- *Lilly's Purple Plastic Purse* (taking responsibility)
- *Do Unto Otters: A Book about Manners* (Golden Rule)

Take advantage of teachable moments

While it is beneficial to talk about soft skills with your kids, they will learn best when they experience character building situations. We only truly learn patience when we are placed in a scenario where we must be patient. We learn kindness when we are in a position where we have to share something we want for ourselves.

Since it is best when the experiences are genuine, think of different scenarios where your child might have to demonstrate desired behaviors in real life situations. Stay attuned to daily activities and actions to take advantage of any opportunity to teach your little one lessons about character.

Encourage good behavior

Foster growth with positive feedback and be specific with the words you use when offering praise. Words like "good job" and "you're so smart" can be empty and nebulous to kids. Instead, state how they are persistent problem solvers when looking for a puzzle piece. Talk about how you thought it was kind to share a toy during a play date. When you praise in this manner, you help children to see themselves as capable of learning and growing. Be quick to express your joy and be sure to explain the meaning of the words you use, to help expand their vocabulary.

Positive reinforcement strategies, such as sticker charts, will also help to promote good behaviors. As we said before, our daughter is responsible for age-appropriate household tasks. When we first introduced these chores, we posted a "chore chart" on our refrigerator. She helped make the chart and pick out the graphics for each activity. By involving her in this part, it gave her ownership and built anticipation.

We expected her to complete tasks without fussing and without being reminded multiple times. Each time she would do one of her chores, we would celebrate by putting a sticker in the appropriate place on the chart. This type of incentive helped to get her excited about tasks and fostered an immediate sense of accomplishment. She came to understand her role in the family, and it didn't take much time before we no longer had to utilize the chart.

Be clear with expectations and follow through

You can foster an effective transition into kindergarten if you are able to identify and establish expectations in your home. When you create household rules, your children will better function in the classroom setting because they will begin to learn about routine and structure. Therefore, it is important to regularly discuss your expectations and explain why you require certain behaviors. Then consistently follow through with consequences when your preschoolers disobey.

Our daughter was once throwing a bouncy ball in our house, and we asked her to stop. We set a clear guideline (you can roll the ball on the floor, but you can't throw it), and explained why throwing the ball in the air might lead to the destruction of something. Then we taught her what it looked like to roll it on the floor with a demonstration, and told her we would take the ball away if she threw it again (and we would have followed through if she had).

The difficult part is usually our inability to consistently follow through—and we've all heard (or been) that parent. We once were at a pool, and a mother threatened little Johnny that, if he didn't stop running around the pool, she would take him home. After Johnny did it a couple more times and the parent continued to lob empty threats, Johnny learned very quickly that words didn't matter. Kids are smart. They realize when parents are simply making hollow remarks. And eventually, they won't respond appropriately because the threats, in reality, are meaningless.

The next time you require a certain behavior, be sure the consequence is one in which you will definitely be able to follow through. So many times we hear parents threaten consequences, and then when the child disobeys or exhibits inappropriate behavior, no penalties are implemented. We probably wouldn't want to leave the pool either, so maybe we would require him to sit next to us for five minutes if he ran again.

In other words, don't make a threat in the heat of the moment that you won't be able or willing to carry out. Try to avoid reactive responses and the tendency to simply yell when children disobey. Instead, proactively discuss expectations and consequences (positive or negative) in advance.

Other important aspects of setting clear expectations include teaching a child to accept the word "no" and to obey quickly. All kids seem to go through a phase where they argue, delay their response, or test boundaries. While they might not give an outright defiant response, they might use tactics to avoid obeying. Our daughter attempted to create distractions, or she frequently asked one question after another to delay.

A child who doesn't accept "no" from a parent has the potential to become a student—and later an employee—who doesn't have a proper respect for authority. The reality is, students in school, employees in the workplace, and citizens of a society will not always be able to insist on their own way.

Be patient and persistent

We first started to teach our daughter to say "please" when she wanted something when she was about two years old. It literally took us at least a year before she began to say please on a regular basis. Even then, she didn't say it all the time. But when she demandingly asked for something during that period, we would patiently say to her, "How do you ask nicely?" We would try our best to respond to her improper behavior without fail and without getting angry.

As parents, it is so easy to let inappropriate actions slide on occasion, but to most effectively foster growth we must be persistent. Kids almost always respond best when parents themselves are able to relentlessly react to a child's poor behavior with a proper tone. Often a change in tone on our part can de-escalate a tense situation.

In the midst of a conflict, try to take a deep breath, get down on the floor with your child, hold her in your lap (if she will let you) and speak quietly into her ear. You may be surprised at how quickly you can turn a hard situation into a precious one.

Common sense isn't common anymore

You will help prepare your preschooler to succeed in school if you proactively instill virtue, good character, and a positive attitude. Early elementary school teachers strive to create an environment described in this chapter, so give your child a head start by doing the same in your home. Incorporate practices into your family's everyday events that nurture healthy dispositions and interpersonal skills. Just as you develop your kids' cognitive abilities, develop character and you will foster a readiness to learn in any setting, including a structured classroom.

This may all sound like common sense, but unfortunately, educators often have to face classrooms where many students frequently exhibit poor behavior. Surely, a teacher's job is to develop students' character as well as their minds, but all care-givers have to be intentional about teaching these lessons. It will require patience, consistency, perseverance, and repeated opportunities to instill positive traits and attitudes. Regardless of academic aptitude or existing knowledge prior to kinder-garten, children who possess soft skills are much more likely to thrive in life.

9

How a Child Develops

What is usually the first word a baby will utter? If you think it is either "ma ma" or "da da," you are probably correct. And there are two reasons for this. First, because babies are developmentally capable of saying these two sounds. Second, because these are typically the words they hear most frequently early in life.

Infants, toddlers, and preschoolers all develop at different times. Just as some babies begin to crawl earlier than others, some toddlers will learn numbers, letters, and other cognitive functions more quickly. In fact, developmental psychologists believe young children are often forced to learn concepts before they are ready, which could actually harm them in the long term.[1] For that reason, try not to compare your kids' abilities with others or force learning when they aren't measuring up. Instead, create an environment where each individual will grow at his or her own pace.

One of the most powerful ways to develop infant, toddler, and preschoolers' social skills, cognitive abilities, and personal attributes is through experience and the culture of their home. Plenty of interaction with parents, relatives, friends, and other children can be an effective way of developing skills and intellectual functions.

This was definitely true for our two-year-old. Because we were providing child care to a friend's toddler who was a year older, our own child's vocabulary expanded greatly. She was regularly interacting with someone who had a much more developed vocabulary.

Thousands of teachers and preschools in the United States utilize a strategy known as the Montessori Method. These Montessori schools are popular—and effective—for a couple of reasons. First, the teachers value the importance of each individual child. They adapt instruction based on each student's needs and previous learning experiences.

Second, after providing initial structure and direction, the schools give preschoolers the freedom to explore and learn at their own pace.[2] Young kids have an innate desire to learn and master skills, and adults simply need to provide the resources and tools to foster growth. Perhaps more than any other time period, children from birth through age six absorb a ton of information. Therefore, let your children explore their surroundings through repeated exercises and activities.

Since young children have brains like sponges, do you encourage or discourage the seemingly nonstop "why" questions they ask? It was determined that young children with inquisitive minds ask an average of 76 questions per hour.[3] If you do the math, that means they ask about 900 questions every day! It is important to understand that the questioning is a critical process in their cognitive development. Each time kids ask a "why" question they are probing, making connections, developing understandings, identifying patterns, and learning new concepts.

Growing a young child's brain

Environmental factors are especially important during the early years of growth. If there is a lack of needed stimuli during that time, then children may not reach their full potential.[4] So be sure to create an atmosphere which offers ample opportunities for your children to build knowledge. Try to spark interest in ideas and encourage them to wonder: How do things work? What does that mean? What causes that? What can I control? What happens if...? This is how a child's brain develops. Children build knowledge and learn basic concepts by investigating the world and by internalizing questions such as these.

You already know kids like to imitate adults and peers. Take advantage of that and sing the ABC song, use whole sentences when speaking, and include math conversations regularly. They will rapidly acquire complex abilities and develop language skills simply by hearing your voice and imitating your words and actions.[5] As little ones develop skills and abilities, remember to foster a sense of self pride for their accomplishments.

Cognitive development occurs when children are free to independently build knowledge and with guided social interactions. Whether they learn on their own or in a social setting, it is important to note their cognitive capabilities. From age zero to 24 months, infants and toddlers use motor activities, their eyes, ears, and other senses to develop an understanding of their environment.

Between the ages of two and seven the ability to think logically is lacking, but toddlers and preschoolers are better able to problem solve, articulate their experiences, and represent their world with language, symbols, pictures, and actions. They are more creative and able to use dolls, toy kitchen sets, dress-up clothes, miniature cars, and other props to "make believe."[6]

It is important for parents to learn when each individual child is able to develop particular capacities with proper support. Therefore, we encourage moms and dads to take the time and effort to see what children are capable of learning by continually exposing them to academic ideas and experiences.

During our daughter's early toddler years, she often enjoyed dressing her dolls. However, at first, she was unable to put the shirt over the doll's head or put the doll's legs into the pants. As I (Annie) sat with her, demonstrated strategies, provided guidance, and encouraged her, she was soon able to dress the dolls by herself. Her abilities with this specific task developed through collaboration and cooperation. Caregivers who interact with children in this manner will find out what kids are capable of learning.

Well known educational psychologist, Lev Vygotsky, represented this idea with the Venn diagram below. As you can see, kids will be able to learn and master some skills on their own. But there are other things they won't be able to do or learn because they simply don't yet have the developmental capabilities.

The key is the area where the two circles overlap, which is known as the Zone of Proximal Development. When parents understand what a child can learn with appropriate support, they will foster growth.

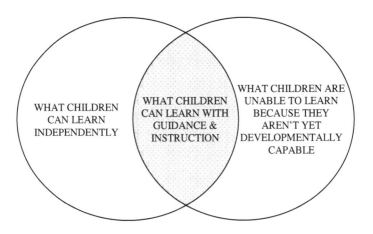

To further extend this idea, be sure to start with easy tasks and then eventually move toward more complex ones. If you find that your child is unable to master something, make the task even easier.

For instance, see if your toddler can count to five with your guidance and help. If she is skipping numbers or can't remember the proper order after attempting it a few times, then ask her to count to three instead. If that still doesn't work, then perhaps she isn't developmentally ready. Simply come back to it at a more optimal time. Try it again a week or month later and you may experience success the second time around.

Here are additional examples of each of the three zones.

Drawing pictures (2 – 3 years old)

Can do independently:
Draw scribbles that may or may not look like a face.

Can do if guided (Zone of Proximal Development):
Draw a picture of a face, which includes a mouth, eyes, and a nose after Mom shows how to draw a big circle for the head, small circles for the eyes and nose, and a line for the mouth.

Can't do even if guided:
Draw with accuracy and detail.

Motor skills (3 years old)

Can do independently:
Throw a Frisbee without proper form.

Can do if guided (Zone of Proximal Development):
Throw a Frisbee with proper form after Dad shows how to hold it and then directs the child's arm in the proper throwing motion.

Can't do even if guided:
Regularly throw a Frisbee with accuracy.

Literacy (3 years old)

Can do independently:
Trace letters.

Can do if guided (Zone of Proximal Development):
Mom demonstrates the strokes to make a letter and the child writes the letter underneath.

Can't do even if guided:
Spell a word.

Once children master new skills and develop knowledge (with or without parental support), it is also important to continually circle back to the learning. Ask elementary school teachers if kids forget and they will definitely answer yes! Toddlers and preschoolers are no different. They need continual exposure to help learn and remember. For example, if you recently began teaching your children basic shapes such as circles, triangles, and squares, then be sure to come back to these regularly to see if they can recognize them again in future play sessions.

Don't put a timeline on learning and don't be surprised if your kids forget something you thought they knew. Play with the shapes in different contexts, and know that repetition will eventually result in mastery.

Social-emotional development

To raise flourishing children, we must be sure to develop more than just their brains. It is equally important to help them relate well with others and properly manage and express emotions. In fact, social-emotional and cognitive development go hand in hand. Preschoolers who build self-confidence and learn positive social skills are more likely to be successful learners later on.[7] But kids won't learn these skills on their own. Parents and caregivers have to teach young people how to develop healthy, positive relationships. They have to proactively nurture self-esteem, self-awareness, and self-control.

To foster self-esteem, encourage your child to try new tasks and then gently challenge him to persist until completion if he faces difficulties along the way. If you know he has the capacity to accomplish a certain goal, then don't let him give up. Giving up is a learned habit, one that gets easier each time he does it. If he does face hurdles, teach him to be patient and discuss his emotions when he gets frustrated or upset.

Also, don't be afraid to let your children fail every once in a while. Of course, you don't want to create a situation where failure will harm them, but overcoming failures (that only have minor consequences) and using failure as a learning experience is one of the most powerful ways to develop a healthy self-esteem. When our daughter was two, she tried to balance an irregularly shaped toy on a small block. She was unable to come up with a solution and I (Jeff) couldn't make it work either. I simply had to teach her to accept the outcome. This resulted in crying because she was determined to balance the toy, but she learned that not all things are possible.

You will cultivate self-confidence when you give preschoolers a sense of responsibility and control with daily tasks. Let them see the value of working alone and allow them to figure things out without adult intervention. When our daughter was old enough to pick up toys on her own, it was a difficult transition from having Mommy's help to taking responsibility for cleaning up. It took some convincing that, as a big girl, she now had the capacity to make sure her space was picked up before bedtime.

Certainly, she still needed to be guided. I (Annie) would ask her what she wanted to clean up first and where her toys should go. Then I would make a game out of it, seeing how quickly she could get tasks done. She would report to me that the first task was done and then I would set her on the next chore. I would check her progress, remind her of what she missed, and praise her for being such a big, responsible girl. After cleaning up the entire mess she was very proud of herself, since she had completed the task on her own.

To promote self-awareness, identify traits unique to your child. Talk about her pretty blue eyes, her strong legs, her inquisitive mind, her love of a certain activity, or any other special characteristics. Frequently discuss her interests, thoughts, preferred activities, and feelings. Talk about her emotions and why they may or may not make sense or truly align with the situation.

There was one instance where I (Jeff) observed a child screaming incessantly because she thought her daddy was getting hurt while wrestling with an old college friend. The dad had to explain to his daughter that they were simply playing. There was no reason to get upset. In this case, the child did not fully understand the situation and a simple conversation helped to calm emotions.

Once children reach the late toddler stage, they are increasingly able to use words to describe their thoughts. At that point, help them to become more self aware by asking questions like, "Why are you so upset?" "What makes you smile?" "Was that task easy for you?" "How are you different than your friends?"

Another major component of a child's social-emotional development includes the ability to self-regulate and control emotions. You can cultivate self-control by teaching seven things.

1. **Talk about different emotions.** The emojis on your phone are great because you can help your toddler identify the faces that represent different emotions. You can use these pictures as a springboard to explain what it means to be scared, excited, joyful, confused, or any other sentiment.

2. **Teach young children to express emotions in appropriate ways.** Outbursts can be frequent, but challenge them to alter their behavior when it is inappropriate. If your toddler whines or stomps his feet in defiance, encourage him to use his words to express his thoughts instead.

3. **Follow daily routines.** Get to a point where your child can switch between activities with minimal guidance or direction.

4. **Help preschoolers make appropriate choices.** If unable to make a good choice, offer two or three options acceptable to you and require your children to pick one. If they make a bad choice, discuss the con-

sequences of that choice. In life, whether as a child or an adult, most of our choices have some sort of consequence, good or bad. Teach this valuable life lesson early on.

5. **Teach kids to follow rules.** Provide reasons for the rules you or others have created, and explain that when rules are broken, there are consequences. Somewhere between the ages of 12 and 18 months, our child began to understand our expectations and obey them.

6. **Encourage respectful behaviors.** Especially be considerate of other people's property and materials. Whenever we visited Grandma's house we had to model how to hold the fragile, stuffed animals correctly.

7. **Increase their ability to delay gratification.** Provide opportunities where a prize will be received only after completing a long-term task.

A final area of concern as it relates to social development is perhaps the most obvious: Teaching toddlers and preschoolers how to build healthy relationships with others. Start by making it a priority to spend time with friends, extended family, and other children. Introduce your little one to new people and unfamiliar settings.

Our family travels quite a bit during the summer, and we often attend church wherever we are visiting. We put our daughter in the kids' program at the church to help her learn to play and talk with kids she doesn't know. Some children will immediately jump right in and start playing with others, while some will take their time. At first our daughter was very hesitant to interact with people she didn't know, but with continued opportunities she got better at meeting and interacting with new friends.

It is interesting to note that about 40% of the children easily adapt to new experiences, 15% adjust slowly, and 10% take quite a bit of effort to adjust to a new setting. The remaining 35% were a mix depending on the situation.[8] So don't worry, it is completely normal if your child seems shy around others.

Toddlers will often play beside friends instead of with each other, and they will spend a lot of time making observations. This behavior is developmentally appropriate. We could never get our toddler to eat in a restaurant because she would be so intent on watching other babies at nearby tables.

When kids do start playing with each other, teach them how to compromise, take turns, and problem solve. Offer support to help resolve conflicts, and encourage cooperation in a way that helps them achieve common goals.

Quarrels are to be expected, but the good news is that disagreements are often very short and quickly forgotten. If there is a social conflict, below is a problem solving strategy we like to employ (and many elementary school teachers use a similar model). Sometimes children don't know how to put their frustrations into words in a way that helps the situation, so teach a basic script. This provides words to help communicate feelings and discuss what needs to be done.

- I don't like it when...
- It makes me feel...
- Next time can you please...
- Say you are sorry for what you did.
- Talk about what you will do differently next time.

Here's what it could look like. One child says to another: "I don't like it when you grab a toy out of my hand. It makes me feel angry and sad. Can you please ask me first next time?" The offending child says: "I'm sorry for grabbing your toy and hurting your feelings. Next time I will ask if we can play together." As a kindergarten teacher, I (Annie) would make sure my students had tried this strategy first before intervening. If one came up to me saying, "Sally took my book right out of my hand," I would ask if they had tried working it out together.

Obviously, some conflicts require more intervention, but this script worked often enough to be effective, and it encouraged autonomy and responsibility. This process will have to be modeled and practiced repeatedly using various scenarios before children can do it on their own.

When you teach cooperation and model the importance of working together, your children will develop kind, respectful, affirming, caring, and pleasing relationships. Additionally, they will start to show empathy and concern for the needs of others.

When our three-year-old daughter had a rare chance to play with her cousin who lived 600 miles away, it took time for them to interact and develop a relationship. At the end of our visit, it was incredibly heartwarming when our niece gave her a Minnie Mouse toy phone. It was such a precious display of care and concern given how much our daughter loved Minnie. Your kids will do the same if you offer similar types of opportunities.

As you can see, interactions with other children and adults can have an enormous influence on your child's development. It is important to remember that children will reach social-emotional milestones and abilities at different ages, but the following provides you with a general timeline of what to expect.[9]

Birth – 2 months

Your infant has two states:
- Attraction to pleasant stimulus
- Withdrawal from unpleasant situations

2 – 5 months

Your children will develop the ability to:
- Match the expressions of caregivers.
- Respond to others' expressions, such as smiling.
- Wave arms and legs to communicate excitement.
- Laugh at external stimuli.

- Smile when looking in the mirror.
- Express sadness.

6 – 12 months

Your children will develop the ability to:
- Express additional emotions such as fear, anger, and separation anxiety.
- Begin to understand parents' facial expressions and make meaning of them.
- Show more comfort around the people they know, and anxiety around those they don't know.
- Increase exploration (when they feel secure).
- Attach to familiar adults.

13 – 18 months

Your children will develop the ability to:
- Play at an increased level with familiar family members and friends.
- Become more self-aware.
- Follow simple rules and commands.

19 – 24 months

Your children will develop the ability to:
- Improve self-regulation.
- Develop additional emotions, such as pride, embarrassment, guilt, empathy, joy, and guilt.
- Be more tolerant of the absence of primary caregivers.
- Increase self-control.

2 – 4 years old

Your children will develop the ability to:
- Improve self-esteem.
- Understand cause and effect.
- Increase interactive play with others.
- Better comprehend the intentions of others.
- Understand the cause of others' emotions.

5 – 6 years old

Your children will develop the ability to:
- Interpret, predict, and influence others' emotional reactions.
- Be more reliant upon words to express emotions.
- Improve problem solving skills.
- Understand the purpose of rules.

Creating a culture of learning

Possibly the most important factor to a child's cognitive and social-emotional development is the culture and climate you create in your home. It isn't time at preschool, or hours of schooling once they reach elementary school.

In actuality, children spend most of their time with parents, siblings, and friends. If you run the numbers, from birth to age 18, kids are in school only about 15 – 20% of their life. They are sleeping for quite a bit of time, which then leaves about 40 – 50% of life with family and community members.

Here are the top things caregivers can do to create an environment of growth.

- Be aware of peer interactions. If your toddler's friend screams when she doesn't get something, then your toddler will likely adopt a similar behavior.
- Allow for creativity.
- Incorporate play with a variety of materials (e.g., rocks, sticks, toys, dolls, clay, or many other objects you possess in and around your home).
- Continually comment on the actions you observe: "I like how you shared." "Take turns with that toy." "Let her play with that first." "You made a kind choice." "I like how you asked for my advice."
- Ask questions: Who, what, when, where, how, why, what if?
- Point out positive and negative behaviors.

- Make connections between previous experiences and new knowledge.
- Explain what good behavior looks like and then encourage proper actions.
- Encourage your little ones to seek assistance from adults when appropriate.

Kids will learn by what they hear and see, so we would be remiss if we didn't again stress the importance of limiting television viewing and screen time. Many shows do not deal with social-emotional issues properly, and your children often develop inappropriate social responses because of what they watch. If you do allow your child to watch television programs, then be sure to prescreen them to ensure age-appropriate content.

There are many broadcasts that actually teach proper social behavior, and they will be of greater benefit if parents talk with children regarding what is seen on the screen. Furthermore, learning is solidified when caregivers connect television programs with everyday experiences. For example, we once saw an exhibit on butterflies at our local nature center. Later, while watching a documentary on the same topic, we were able to tie together what we learned at the exhibit with the documentary.

In sum, identify what is developmentally appropriate by continually providing different experiences and by teaching your young kids new academic content. Even if they aren't ready to master a concept or skill, try it anyway. Oftentimes, simple exposure (without striving for mastery) is beneficial. Be patient. While some abilities and skills will develop more gradually, some will simply emerge at a given—and perhaps surprising—time. Support from and interaction with parents, siblings, family members, and friends will be the conduit through which children's cognitive abilities and social emotional growth will strengthen during the early years.

10

Preschool & Beyond

We often feel pressure to make sure our children have a strong academic foundation. Some of that pressure is necessary because it motivates us to be intentional, thoughtful, and wise. But sometimes it can be negative. For instance, a number of caregivers feel as though toddlers should enter some form of early educational program at two and three years old.

No doubt, young children's learning before they enter kindergarten is essential for later school success, but that learning can happen in informal settings as effectively as in a formal educational setting. Parents and caregivers should not feel pressured to enroll their kids because other parents are doing it, or because an "expert" from an Internet search says we should.

If you decide preschool is not for your family, we feel that the ideas presented in this book, paired with opportunities for social engagement, will set your children up for success. We hope we have definitively explained the crucial role parents play. We hope this book has equipped you to educate toddlers and preschoolers so they are ready for school and for everyday interactions. We also hope you will consider the ideas that follow when deciding on the best approach regarding early educational experiences.

Should children attend preschool?

Early schooling is important, but that does not necessarily mean all kids should enroll in a local preschool. In fact, some programs don't focus enough on social-emotional growth. Others aren't developmentally appropriate and have a tendency to push students academically too early, causing more harm than good in the long run.[1]

In contrast, effective educational experiences allow children to take initiative in their own learning. Kids are encouraged to play and actively engage with the academic content discussed in the previous chapters. This can happen in a quality preschool setting or in the home.

The question of whether your child should attend preschool prior to kindergarten is not always an easy one and is certainly not one other people can answer for you. Consider your own situation and think about the many variables at play.

- What does your weekly social interaction look like? Are you going to play groups together, or is your child staying with a caregiver (grandparents, family members, friends, Sunday school child care)?
- Does a parent stay home full time? Do you have time to devote to intentional play, interactions, and experiences?
- Do you have a flourishing preschool in your area? If yes, what are the costs?
- Is your child ready for a more formal school setting? Trust your gut and if you feel he or she isn't ready, delay the decision for a year.
- Do both parents work? If yes, a high quality preschool program might offer a richer experience than a day care setting.

Professional opinion regarding an early education in a formal setting ranges widely. The right age to start and what it should look like are heavily debated topics. Ultimately, you know your child and your lifestyle best. Children can gain all the skills they would acquire in preschool in a healthy, thriving household. If you use this book as a guide, your kids will thrive in kindergarten.

Don't stress about getting it exactly right. Understand best practices, understand your children, and make an informed decision. Be watchful and be willing to make adjustments. Stay involved and advocate for them whether they are enrolled in preschool or not.

Though many of her friends did attend, we didn't send our daughter to our local preschool (which was offered for both three- and four-year-olds). There were a few reasons for this. First, I (Annie) had the time and knowledge necessary to effectively provide early educational experiences. (Of course, we've been passing that knowledge to you throughout this book, so you now have the requisite information as well.)

Second, she and I had an active social life. With play dates, play groups, and child care at church, she regularly engaged in a wide range of social interactions. Third, and probably most important, I wasn't ready to send her off to preschool at age three. I knew she would have many opportunities to learn in a more formal setting later, but as a three- and four-year-old, I wanted her mom and dad to be the primary voices in her life.

And let me tell you, the payoff was rich. The delight she and I both found during our learning experiences together was priceless. Tears clouded my vision as I witnessed her growth, and I felt privileged to have had a front row seat to her development.

In place of a formal preschool setting, I structured experiential and learning sessions every week day, with each session lasting approximately two hours. It wasn't very rigorous or overly controlled, but I was deliberate about spending the time. I provided opportunities for her to actively engage with the ideas included in this book, and I taught her skills, concepts, and knowledge in all areas—including math, science, literacy, social studies, physical education, and the arts. While much learning took place from the time she was an infant, we didn't start this more formal structure until she was four years old.

Even though we chose to provide our own educational experiences for our child before kindergarten, if circumstances had been different, we wouldn't have hesitated to enroll her in a local preschool. If you decide to send your kids to preschool based on your own situation, the most effective programs will:

- Develop the whole child—including physical, social-emotional, and character development.
- Focus on the arts and sciences in equal measure with reading, writing, and math.
- Foster creativity and a spirit of inquiry.
- Develop communication, problem solving, and critical thinking skills.
- Develop a sense of cooperation among students and teachers.
- Strive to develop caring, respectful relationships.
- Offer guided lessons while also providing ample time for individual play and exploration.
- Have a student to teacher ratio not greater than 10:1.
- Set high standards (that are developmentally appropriate).
- Meet the individual needs of each student and create student-specific goals.
- Have a wealth of educational resources.
- Have clear and consistent behavioral standards for all students.
- Promote understanding, open dialogue, and diversity of thought.
- Encourage parental involvement.
- Hire highly qualified teachers and maintain state licensure requirements.

Based on this list of criteria, we recommend sending children to a Montessori preschool. While each school is different, a Montessori education best captures the needs of young learners. Each child is valued, students actively build knowledge through play and exploration, and there is a proper balance between self-directed learning and teacher guidance.[2]

If there are other options available in your area, here are some additional questions you can ask providers to get an idea of the preschool's effectiveness.

- What educational resources and activities do teachers utilize?
- What does a typical day look like?
- How do teachers handle behavioral issues?
- What content is stressed in class?
- What is the educational philosophy of the school?
- When and how do teachers communicate with parents?
- What are the school's rules?

It is also helpful to ask neighboring parents and visit potential educational institutions. Check to see if the facility is clean, organized, and safe. Walk into a classroom and see if it is full of books, equipment, and other resources. If class is in session, observe how teachers interact with the students. Find out if there is something unique or special about the school and determine if it is a proper fit for your children. Find a good match and the experience will likely prepare them for kindergarten.

The structures and systems of a kindergarten classroom

As your child's preschool years come to an end, it's time to begin thinking about kindergarten. While speaking to parents of incoming kindergartners, I (Annie) would tell them what to expect during the year, explaining how kindergarten is about academics, social-emotional development, and character building. It's about fostering an environment where students feel safe to ask questions, experiment, and fail. I would tell parents about the importance of creating a classroom community that works together for the good of the group.

One year, a parent commented on how it was his job to foster an emotionally stable child. Of course, I agree. Stability should come from the home. But to be an effective teacher, I had to see my students as little people with needs and emotions, not just as recipients of information.

As parents of incoming kindergartners, continue to focus on developing every facet of your child's life. Strive to inspire a lifelong learner who will find solutions, be respectful, and put others first. In the months leading up to the first day of kindergarten, have multiple conversations about these goals and expectations together. If children have an idea of what to expect before arriving, they will better respond to all the various circumstances in class.

Kindergarten teachers expect their students to be able to assimilate into their classroom, follow the classroom rules, and learn how to be a student. Educators strive to develop an excitement about new ideas and they work hard to create a culture of cooperation, exploration, and discovery. As children settle into a new school year, it takes some time to learn the routines, but eventually they internalize the classroom expectations and build stamina for a busy day.

One of the first discussions I had as a teacher with kindergarteners was about the systems of our class and why we needed them. Students should understand that parameters are established to create structure, to optimize learning, and to help our classroom function smoothly for everyone's benefit. Each learning area (e.g., tables, centers, whole group mat, and hallways) had different procedures that I would walk through and practice with my students. For example, one of the first structures I taught was how to properly behave when sitting on the mat, which is where they received much of their direct instruction. They had to follow five rules.

1. Sit with legs crossed.

2. Hands in lap.
3. Eyes on the speaker.
4. Ears listening.
5. Mouth closed.

When children follow directions and care about those around them, they begin to understand their role in the community. Students ought to learn when it's time to sit still and listen and when it's appropriate to engage in conversation or learn through play.

The spring and summer before kindergarten

Now it's time to prepare your child (and you) for the first day of school. Begin by learning all you can about your local school district. Do you have an option to send your child to more than one school? If yes, are there a limited number of seats for students? What are the school's policies and procedures? If necessary, what are the procedures for transportation to and from school? Is there a registration deadline? (Most districts require you to register your child in the spring of the previous school year.) What forms are you required to complete? What immunizations are mandatory before the first day? What types of food services does the school offer? What is the yearly and daily schedule for kindergarten children?

Most districts offer some sort of orientation meeting to provide a description of the kindergarten program and answer many of these questions. Call your local school, add it to your calendar, and make it a priority to attend.

In addition to the orientation, districts typically have a kindergarten visitation day to provide both parents and students the opportunity to become familiar with the school. Make it a point to visit and learn the principal's name and the name of your child's teacher. (Don't forget to talk about how to properly address school officials.) Walk the school's hall-ways to learn where various rooms are located. Walk into your child's future classroom, the library, the gym, and the cafeteria. Learn as much as you can about the teacher's classroom expectations and behavioral standards. Also be sure to share your enthusiasm regarding all the great things about school. Each day is filled with so much learning and fun social interactions!

The very first day of kindergarten is always so exciting and I (Annie) remember the buzz filling the hallways. The day was filled with anticipation as well as some trepidation by students, parents, and teachers alike. The many unknowns facing all involved had everyone's heart beating just a little bit faster. So it's not unusual for kindergarten students to cling to Mom or Dad a little more tightly on the first day (or during the entire first week).

Procedures vary from school to school, but the system my district utilized worked well to help calm everyone. Before the first day of classes, the kindergarten students and parents had a scheduled opportunity to visit my classroom to introduce themselves and drop off school supplies. I had places in the room for students to put materials so they had a chance to explore the room with the comfort of Mom or Dad at their side.

On the very first school day, students lined up outside where I would greet them. I gave each child a specific spot to line up because they would begin every subsequent school day at the same spot. Once the first bell rang, we would all wave our goodbyes to the parents and then proceed down the hallway to our classroom. If a student was unwilling to let go, I would gently take his hand and he would help me lead the class to our room. I reassured Mom or Dad that if there continued to be an issue, I would call. However, it was important to have a clean break at the door of the building.

It was essential for the normal routines to begin the first day so students can learn what is expected of them and feel a sense of independence. This type of opportunity goes a long way in familiarizing a child with a new setting. Preparing your student for the first day by telling her what is going to happen and what to do if she is uncertain or afraid will help her feel more comfortable. Make a big deal of being a big, brave girl, and when she comes home after the first day, celebrate her accomplishments.

Stay involved

Once your children are enrolled in school, don't underestimate your role. Parental involvement makes a huge difference. Continue to be a part of your students' education from kindergarten all the way through high school. In fact, family involvement and the environment you create in your home can have a far greater influence on your children's academic success than the quality of their school and even the quality of their teachers.[3] In other words, foster a culture of learning and growth in your home throughout all of life.

Here are some practical ways parents can help kids be more successful while in elementary, middle, and high school.

- **Communicate high expectations.** Encourage hard work, teach discipline, and discuss the importance of an education. Of anything we mention in this section, this is one of the most important ways to stay involved.[4] However, be sure to create a loving atmosphere where your kids don't feel overly pressured to succeed.
- **Communicate with your child's teachers.** Go to parent-teacher conferences, send an occasional email to check on progress, and learn how you can come alongside your son or daughter to help.
- **Help with homework assignments.** This must go beyond setting rules to ensure your children get the homework done. Take the time to sit with them and help out as they complete school tasks. Ask many questions to ensure understanding or to expand knowledge. If you are unsure of how to answer a question or complete a math problem, do a Google search and watch a video

alongside your son or daughter. There are many great resources—Khan Academy, PhET Simulations from the University of Colorado, and BrainPOP are a few examples of helpful websites.

- **Check out available resources on the school's website.** See if your child's teacher has a web page, it often contains helpful information.
- **Continue to provide educational experiences in your home.** Remember, teachers often have up to 25 – 30 students in class, so extra one-on-one time at home will be of benefit.
- **Do all you can to ensure that your kids get to school every day.** There is no doubt about it—school attendance correlates with academic success.[5]
- **Be a part of the school community.** Introduce yourself to other parents and educational leaders, attend school functions, and volunteer at the school.

Don't stop working with your kids when they start school. Always be a teacher as well as a parent. Your children will indeed make greater gains in the classroom if you stay involved, set high standards, and communicate the value of lifelong learning.

Fostering growth from birth

A young brain takes in everything, so whether you provide an early childhood education in your home or at a preschool, don't underestimate the ability of your child's mind. Through everyday interactions, activities, and the natural trial and error of play, kids are continually acquiring knowledge and skills.

You don't have to get complicated. You don't have to buy a lot of stuff. You simply need to create an environment that values learning and growth. So be intentional about your actions. Take the time to have conversations with your kids. Teach them how to work effectively with others. Provide a language-rich environment. Visit educational institutions such as libraries, museums, and parks. Through repeated exposure and these types of deliberate routines, young children will develop and better understand their environment and the world.

We regularly asked our preschooler questions such as, "How was your day?" "What was your favorite part of the day?" "Who did you play with and what did you do?" (We made sure to ask questions that required more than one word answers.) She wasn't able to answer many of our questions when she was a toddler, but with time and practice she was able to string together a growing series of words. Eventually, she was able to respond with complete sentences. As we continued to inquire about everyday events, she also got better at including more depth and detail.

With all learning experiences, create a no-pressure environment. Don't be tempted to push anything your kids aren't interested in. Instead, let them be your guide regarding when to participate in a given educational task. If they are disinterested or get discouraged, set the activity aside and revisit it another time. There are enough academic pressures later in school, especially with so many state-mandated tests. Let your children enjoy their preschool years and strive to create a sense of happiness and well-being.

Enjoy playing and interacting with your infant, toddler, and preschooler. Cultivate positive character traits, ask questions, indulge their curiosity, and go into depth with information. Turn daily events into learning opportunities and build on the spontaneity of teachable moments. Let your children revel in early educational experiences and watch their eyes light up as they learn.

Suggested Children's Books

Counting Kisses by Karen Katz
Bear Counts by Karma Wilson
One, Two, Three! by Sandra Boynton
Fish Eyes: A Book you can Count On by Lois Ehlert
Chicka, Chicka 1, 2, 3 by Bill Martin Jr. & Michael Sampson
Pumpkin, Pumpkin by Jeanne Titherington
From Head to Toe by Eric Carle
Brown Bear, Brown Bear, What Do You See? by Bill Martin Jr. & Eric Carle
What if Everybody Did That? by Ellen Javernick
One Fish, Two Fish, Red Fish, Blue Fish by Dr. Seuss
The Cat in the Hat by Dr. Seuss
Fox in Socks by Dr. Seuss
Hop on Pop by Dr. Seuss
A, B, C: An Amazing Alphabet Book by Dr. Seuss
Ten Apples up on Top! by Dr. Seuss
Giraffes Can't Dance by Giles Andreae
The Way I Act by Steve Metzger
Bear Says Thanks by Karma Wilson
It's Mine! by Leo Lionni
The Little Red Hen by Carol Ottolenghi
An Awesome Book of Thanks! by Dallas Clayton
Lilly's Purple Plastic Purse by Kevin Henkes
Do Unto Otters: A Book about Manners by Laurie Keller
The Castle Ghost: An Adventure in Great Britain by Walt Disney Company
Goofy Gets in the Act: An Adventure in Australia by Walt Disney Company
Pet Pals: An Adventure in Peru by Walt Disney Company
Goodnight, Daniel Tiger by Angela Santomero
What's Special at Night by Daphne Pendergrass
Daniel Goes to School by Becky Friedman
Daniel Visits the Doctor by Becky Friedman

Notes

Chapter 1 (Setting Your Little One up for Success)

1. Tucker-Drob, Elliot, et al. "Emergence of a Gene x Socioeconomic Status Interaction on Infant Mental Ability between 10 Months and 2 Years." *Psychological Science,* vol. 22, no. 1, 2011.

2. Gutek, Gerald. *Historical and Philosophical Foundations of Education: A Biographical Introduction.* 5th ed., Pearson, 2010.

3. Montessori, Maria, and John Chattin-McNichols. *The Absorbent Mind.* Henry Holt and Company, 1995.

4. Bassok, Daphna, et al. "Is Kindergarten the New First Grade?" *American Education Research Association Open,* vol. 2, no. 1, 2016, 1-31.

5. Ginsburg, Kenneth R. "The Importance of Play in Promoting Healthy Child Development and Maintaining Strong Parent-Child Bonds." *Pediatrics,* vol. 119, no. 1, 2007, pp. 182-91.

6. Cook, Gina, et al. "Fathers' and Mothers' Cognitive Stimulation in Early Play with Toddlers: Predictors of 5th Grade Reading and Math." *Family Science,* vol. 2, no. 2, 2011, pp. 131-45.

7. Honig, Alice S. "Play: Ten Power Boosts for Children's Early Learning." *Young Children,* vol. 62, no. 5, 2007, pp. 72-8.

8. Suskind, Dana. *Thirty Million Words: Building a Child's Brain.* Dutton, NY, 2015.

9. Baker, Fiona. "Keeping the Roots of Learning Alive with Heuristic Play." *ASCD Express,* vol. 12, no. 10, 2017.

10. The Access Center. "Literacy-Rich Environments." *ReadingRockets.org,* 2014, www.readingrockets.org/article/literacy-rich-environments/. Accessed 11 December 2017.

11. Shonkoff, Jack, and Deborah Phillips, eds. *From Neurons to Neighborhoods: The Science of Early Childhood Development.* National Academy Press, 2000.

12. Luby, Joan, et al. "Maternal Support in Early Childhood Predict Larger Hippocampal Volumes at School Age." *National Academy of Sciences of the United States of America,* vol. 109, no. 2, 2012, pp. 2854-59.

13. "American Academy of Pediatrics Announces New Recommendations for Children's Media Use." *American Academy of Pediatrics.* Oct. 2016, www.aap.org/en-us/about-the-aap/aap-press-room/pages/american-academy-of-pediatrics-announces-new-recommendations-for-childrens-media-use.aspx. Accessed 11 December 2017.

14. Plowman, Lydia, and Joanna McPake. "Seven Myths about Young Children and Technology." *Childhood Education,* vol. 89, no. 1, 2012, pp. 27-33.

15. Martin, Anne, et al. "Specifying the Links between Household Chaos and Preschool Children's Development." *Early Child Development and Care,* vol. 182, no. 10, 2011, pp. 1247-63.

Chapter 2 (Math: It's as Easy as 1, 2, 3)
1. Jacobi-Vessels, Jill, et al. "Teaching Preschoolers to Count: Effective Strategies for Achieving Early Mathematics Milestones." *Early Childhood Education Journal,* vol. 44, no. 1, 2016, pp. 1-9.
2. Claessens, Amy, and Mimi Engel. "How Important Is Where You Start? Early Mathematics Knowledge and Later School Success." *Teachers College Record,* vol. 115, no. 6, 2013.
3. Baroody, Arthur, and Alexis Benson. "Early Number Instruction." *Teaching Children Mathematics,* vol. 8, no. 3, 2001, pp. 154-8.
4. "In a New Survey, Americans say, 'We're Not Good at Math.'" *Changetheequation.org,* http://changetheequation.org/press/new-survey-americans-say-"we're-not-good-math." Accessed 10 June 2017.
5. The National Council of Teachers of Mathematics (*nctm.org*) is an excellent resource to consult when considering what you should teach your preschooler.
6. Gelman, Rochel, and C.R. Gallistel. *The Child's Understanding of Number.* Harvard Press University, 1986.
7. Baroody, Arthur, and Alexis Benson. "Early Number Instruction." *Teaching Children Mathematics,* vol. 8, no. 3, 2001, pp. 154-8.
8. National Research Council. *Learning to Think Spatially.* The National Academies Press, 2006.
9. "Understanding Number Sense." *Math Solutions,* http://mathsolutions.com/making-sense-of-math/number-sense/understanding-number-sense/. Accessed 11 December 2017.
10. Way, Jenni. "Number Sense Series: Developing Early Number Sense." *NRICH enriching mathematics,* February 2011. https://nrich.maths.org/2477. Accessed 11 December 2017.

Chapter 3 (Science: Explore & Discover the World)
1. Bransford, John, and M. Suzanne Donovan, eds. *How Students Learn: Science in the Classroom.* The National Academies Press, 2005.
2. National Research Council. *How People Learn: Brain, Mind, Experience and School.* The National Academies Press, 2000.
3. Copple, Carol, and Sue Bredekamp. *Developmentally Appropriate Practice in Early Childhood Programs: Serving Children from Birth through age,* 3rd ed., National Association for the Education of Young Children, 2009.
4. Trundle, Cathy. "Teaching Science during the Early Childhood Years." *National Geographic Learning,* 2009.

5. Ibid.
6. Ibid.
7. Pine, Karen, et al. "Children's Misconceptions in Primary Science: A Survey of Teachers' Views." *Science and Technological Education,* vol. 19, no. 1, 2010, pp. 79-96.
8. National Research Council. *How People Learn: Brain, Mind, Experience and School.* The National Academies Press, 2000.
9. Katz, Lilian. "STEM in the Early Years." *Early Childhood Research and Practice,* 2010, http://ecrp.uiuc.edu/beyond/seed/katz.html. Accessed 12 December 2017.
10. The National Science Teachers Association (www.nsta.org) has additional process skills and resources available for parents and teachers.

Chapter 4 (Literacy: Laying the Foundation)

1. See www.messforless.net/18-fine-motor-activities-for-preschoolers/ for many more ideas.
2. "Three Tricks to Help Kids Learn to Hold Their Pencil Correctly." *mamaOT,* 2017, http://mamaot.com/3-tricks-to-help-kids-learn-to-hold-their-pencil-correctly/. Accessed 10 June 2017.
3. Bridges, Lois. "What the Research Says: Reading and Writing Connections." *Scholastic,* 2015, http://edublog.scholastic.com/post/what-research-says-reading-and-writing-connections#. Accessed 7 September 2017.
4. Axness, Heli. "Field Notes: Early Learning Planted in Play and Literacy." *ASCD Express,* vol. 12, no. 10, 2017.
5. Haggard, Geraldine. "Setting the Stage for Purposeful Communication: Fostering Emergent Literacy." *Delta Kappa Gamma Bulletin,* vol. 80, no. 3, 2014, pp. 45-8.

Chapter 5 (Social Studies: Understanding Culture & Society)

1. See www.socialstudies.org for many more resources and ideas.
2. Koralek, Derry. "Social Studies from a Sense of Self to a Sense of the World." *Young Children,* vol. 70, no. 3, 2015, pp. 6-9.
3. Ibid.
4. Seefeldt, Carol, et al. *Social Studies for the Preschool/Primary Child.* 8th ed., Prentice Hall, 2010.
5. Melendez, Luisiana. "Using Children's Books as a Social Studies Curriculum Strategy." *Young Children,* vol. 70, no. 3, 2015, pp. 48-53.
6. Epstein, Ann. "Social Studies in Preschool? Yes!" *Young Children,* vol. 69, no. 1, 2014, pp. 78-83.
7. Melendez, Luisiana. "Using Children's Books as a Social Studies Curriculum Strategy." *Young Children,* vol. 70, no. 3, 2015, pp. 48-53.

8. Disney's Small World Library. *The Castle Ghost: An Adventure in Great Britain.* Stoddard, 1991.

9. Zakin, Andrea. "Hand to Hand: Teaching Tolerance and Social Justice One Child at a Time." *Childhood Education,* vol. 88, no. 1, 2012, pp. 3-13.

10. Javernick, Ellen. *What if Everybody Did That?* Two Lions, 2010.

Chapter 6 (Physical Education: Developing Motor & Movement Skills)

1. Timmons, Brian, et al. "Physical Activity for Preschool Children: How Much and How?" *Applied Physiology, Nutrition, and Metabolism,* vol. 32, 2007, pp. 122-34.

2. Son, Seung-Hee, and Samuel Meisels. "The Relationship of Young Children's Motor Skills to Later School Achievement." *Merrill Palmer Quarterly,* vol. 52, no. 4, 2006, pp. 755-78. Cameron, Claire, et al. "Fine Motor Skills and Executive Function Both Contribute to Kindergarten Achievement." *Child Development,* vol. 83, no. 4, 2012, pp. 1229-44.

3. See www.shapeamerica.org for additional resources and ideas.

4. "Physical Activity in Early Childhood: Setting the Stage for Lifelong Healthy Habits." *Centre for Early Childhood Development,* 2011, http://www.excellence-earlychildhood.ca/documents/Parenting 2011 -04.pdf. Accessed 13 December 2017.

5. Pica, Rae. "Learning by Leaps and Bounds. Why Motor Skills Matter." *Young Children,* vol. 63, no. 4, 2008, pp. 48-9.

6. Timmons, Brian, et al. "Physical Activity for Preshool Children: How Much and How?" *Applied Physiology, Nutrition, and Metabolism,* vol. 32, 2007, pp. 122-34.

Chapter 7 (Creative Expression: Fostering Artistic Talent & Appreciation)

1. Eisner, Elliot. "What Can Education Learn from the Arts about the Practice of Education?" *The Encyclopedia of Informal Education,* 2002. www.infed.org/biblio/eisner_arts_and_the_practice_of_education. htm. Accessed 13 December 2017.

2. Jensen, Eric. *Arts with the Brain in Mind.* Association for Supervision and Curriculum, 2001.

3. Wright, Susan. *The Arts, Young Children, and Learning.* Pearson, 2002.

4. Sousa, David. "How the Arts Develop the Young Brain: Neuroscience Research is Revealing the Impressive Impact of Arts Instruction on Students' Cognitive, Social, and Emotional Development." *School Administrator,* vol. 63, no. 11, 2006, pp. 26-32.

5. Parlakian, Rebecca, and Claire Learner. "Beyond Twinkle, Twinkle: Using Music with Infants and Toddlers." *Young Children,* vol. 65, no. 2, 2010, 14-19.

6. Sousa, David. "How the Arts Develop the Young Brain: Neuroscience Research is Revealing the Impressive Impact of Arts Instruction on Students' Cognitive, Social, and Emotional Development." *School Administrator,* vol. 63, no. 11, 2006, pp. 26-32.

7. Shore, Rebecca, and Janis Strasser. "Music for their Minds." *Young Children,* vol. 61, no. 2, 2006, pp. 62-7.

8. Perles, Karen. "Music and Movement: Is it Really that Important?" *brighthubeducation,* 2012, www.brighthubeducation.com/teaching-preschool/47597-importance-of-music-and-movement/. Accessed 13 December 2017.

Chapter 8 (Character Is Higher Than Intellect)

1. Tough, Paul. *How Children Succeed: Grit, Curiosity, and the Hidden Power of Character.* Houghton Mifflin Harcourt, 2012.

2. See Galatians 5:22 and Romans 12 for other biblical character traits.

3. Ramsey, Dave, and Rachel Cruze. *Smart Money Smart Kids.* Lampo Press, 2014.

4. Tough, Paul. *How Children Succeed: Grit, Curiosity, and the Hidden Power of Character.* Houghton Mifflin Harcourt, 2012.

5. Alcorn, Randy. "Combating the Spirit of Entitlement with Gratitude." *eternal perspective ministries,* 2014, www.epm.org/blog/2014/Feb/5/entitlement-gratitude. Accessed 13 December 2017.

6. Duckworth, Angela, and James Gross. "Self-control and Grit: Related but Separate Determinants of Success." *Current Directions in Psychological Science,* vol. 23, no. 5, 2014, pp. 319-30.

7. Laursen, Erik. "The Power of Grit, Perseverance, and Tenacity." *Reclaiming Children and Youth,* vol. 23, no. 4, 2015, pp. 19-24.

8. Duckworth, Angela, and Lauren Eskreis-Winkler. "True Grit." *Observer,* vol. 26, no. 4, 2013.

9. You can go to www.inspirationpeak.com/cgi-bin/poetry.cgi?record =110 to see the entire poem.

10. Radesky, Jenny, et al. "Patterns of Mobile Device Use by Caregivers and Children During Meals in Fast Food Restaurants." *Pediatrics,* vol. 133, no. 4, 2014, pp. 843-9.

Chapter 9 (How a Child Develops)

1. Carlsson-Paige, Nancy, et al. "Reading Instruction in Kindergarten: Little to Gain and Much to Lose." *Allianceforchildhood.org,* 2015.

2. Gutek, Gerald. *Historical and Philosophical Foundations of Education: A Biographical Introduction.* 2nd ed., Prentice Hall, 1997.

3. Kropp, Lisa. "Surprise: It's Stem for Toddlers!" *School Library Journal,* 2015, www.slj.com/2015/07/opinion/first-steps/surprise-its-stem-for-toddlers/. Accessed 13 December 2017.

4. Hadzigeorgiou, Yannis. "A Study of the Development of the Concept of Mechanical Stability in Preschool Children." *Research in Science Education,* vol. 32, no. 3, 2002, pp. 373-91.

5. Berk, Laura, and Adena Meyers. *Infants, Children, and Adolescents.* 8th ed., Pearson, 2015.

6. Snowman, Jack, and Rick McCown. *Psychology Applied to Teaching.* 14th ed., Wadsworth Publishing, 2014.

7. Committee on Integrating the Science of Early Childhood Development. *From Neurons to Neighborhoods: The Science of Early Childhood Development.* National Academies Press, 2000.

8. Berk, Laura, and Adena Meyers. *Infants, Children, and Adolescents.* 8th ed., Pearson, 2015.

9. Ibid.

Chapter 10 (Preschool & Beyond)

1. Marcon, Rebecca. "Moving up the Grades: Relationship between Preschool Model and Later School Success." *Early Childhood Research and Practice,* vol. 4, no. 1, 2002.

2. Check out the American Montessori Society at amshq.org for more information if you are interested.

3. Marzano, Robert. *A New Era of School Reform: Going Where the Research Takes Us.* Mid-continent Research for Education and Learning, Aurora, CO., 2000.

4. Goodwin, Bryan. "The Power of Parental Expectations." *Educational Leadership,* vol. 75, no. 1, 2017, pp. 80-81.

5. Balfanz, Robert and Vaughan Byrnes. *The Importance of Being in School: A Report on Absenteeism in the Nation's Public Schools,* John Hopkins University Center for Social Organization of Schools, 2012.

About the Authors

Jeff Wiesman
Jeff is an associate professor of education at Houghton College, and he teaches courses that focus on how to effectively educate early elementary school students. Before teaching at the university level, Jeff taught mathematics in the public school system for 20 years. He is passionate about creating a fun and engaging culture of learning in his home, and hopes to equip parents to do the same. He enjoys traveling and participating in just about any outdoor activity.

Annie Wiesman
Before becoming a full-time stay-at-home mom, Annie was a kindergarten and first grade teacher for over 8 years. She currently teaches preschool to her daughter, and she writes for the popular parenting website www.babywise.life. Annie enjoys her morning cup of coffee, hiking in the mountains, traveling to see new places, and creating memories together with her family.